Python Challenge:
Learn to program **fast** in

155 Challenges
54 Examples
85 Pages

Published by
PG Online Limited
The Old Coach House
35 Main Road
Tolpuddle
Dorset
DT2 7EW
United Kingdom

sales@pgonline.co.uk
www.pgonline.co.uk
2021

PG ONLINE

All sections

Design and artwork: Jessica Webb / PG Online Ltd
Graphics / images: © Shutterstock

First edition 2021. 10 9 8 7 6 5 4 3 2 1
A catalogue entry for this book is available from the British Library
ISBN: 978-1-910523-35-3
Copyright © PM Heathcote 2021

Printed on FSC® certified paper by Bell and Bain Ltd, Glasgow, UK.

CONTENTS AND CHECKLIST

Start here!
Just follow the line

INTRODUCTION

Learn (through explanations and examples)

- Each new concept, Python statement or programming technique is carefully explained and one or more examples given. All the example programs are given in the **Examples** folder of the free **Python programs** pack (see below), and you can copy, run and edit them if you wish.

Do (with more than 150 challenges)

As each new statement or programming technique is introduced, several practice challenges are given for you to use newly learned skills in writing, editing and running programs.

The challenges are of three different types:

- Short challenges that ask you to write a Python statement or answer a question. You will find the answers to these challenges in the back of the book.

- Challenges that ask you to write and test a program. For these, you need to create your own folder to write, save, edit and run your programs. You could call the folder, for example, **My Python solutions**. You will find suggested solutions to all these challenges in a folder called **Challenge solutions**. This is a subfolder of the **Python programs** folder.

- Challenges that consist of a partially written program for you to complete. These are all identified with a star and are held in a subfolder of the **Python programs** folder called **Starred challenges (incomplete)**. You should download this entire folder to your own computer. When you are ready to do one of these programming challenges, copy the incomplete program to your own folder and rename it, e.g. **Level 1 Challenge 8 (*your initials*).py**. Then complete this program and test it.

  Completed solutions to these partially written programs are also held in the **Challenge solutions** folder. If you get stuck, you can look at the suggested solution, and compare it with yours. There are often several ways of writing correct Python statements to solve the problem, so don't worry if your solution is not identical to the one given. Just make sure yours works correctly!

Review (by selecting topics, regular and starred challenges)

As you work through the book, and the challenges become longer, you will be constantly revisiting statements and techniques you have already covered, using them in different ways. And, if you have already done a Python course and just need to revise what you have already learned, this book is ideal.

! Before you start

Download the free Python programs pack from www.clearrevise.com or www.pgonline.co.uk.

There is a quick reference guide to all of the basic Python syntax at the back of this book. Download and run **syntaxsummary.py** from the **Python programs** folder.

GETTING STARTED

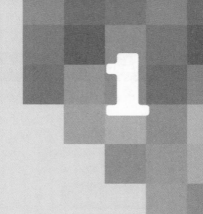

Python is one of the most popular text-based programming languages, widely used in schools and colleges, and also in web development, game development, artificial intelligence, business, computer-aided design and many more applications.

The Python language

Python has two modes of entering and running programs. In **interactive mode**, you can type instructions and Python will respond immediately. This is very useful for trying out statements that you are not sure about, and is a good place to start.

Download Python from **www.python.org/downloads**

> **! Tip**
>
> You cannot save a program that you have written in interactive mode. This has to be done in **script mode**, used in the other levels (or chapters) of this book.

An interactive session

To begin an interactive session, open **Python 3**. On a PC, you can use the **Search** box in the bottom left corner of your screen, or the **Start** menu. Then select the version installed on your computer (e.g. Python 3.9). Load Python's **integrated development environment**, named **IDLE**.

You will see a screen similar to the one below:

```
IDLE Shell 3.9.2                                               —    □    ×
File  Edit  Shell  Debug  Options  Window  Help
Python 3.9.2 (tags/v3.9.2:1a79785, Feb 19 2021, 13:44:55) [MSC v.1928 64 bit (AMD64)] on win32
Type "help", "copyright", "credits" or "license()" for more information.
>>>

                                                                  Ln: 3  Col: 4
```

In this window, which is called the **Python Shell** or **Interactive window**, you can type commands at the >>> prompt.

Example 1

```
>>> print("Hello world")
```

The Python interpreter responds to your command and you will see **Hello world** appear on the next line, followed by a new line with the prompt >>>.

```
Hello world
>>>
```

Output statement (print)

Use the Python Shell (Interactive mode) for Challenges 1–5.

You can use single or double quotes in the **print** statement. If you need speech marks or an apostrophe inside the text to be printed, use single quotes around the whole text to be printed, and double quotes inside it, or vice versa:

Example 2

```
>>> print('The guide told us "Stay very still! " ')
The guide told us "Stay very still! "
```

Example 3

```
>>> print("A gorilla's diet is mainly vegetarian.\
They feed mainly on stems, bamboo shoots and fruits.")
>>>
```

> **! Tip**
>
> If you have a long line of code, you can split it over two lines by typing a backslash (\) and pressing Enter. Then continue the statement on the next line.

When you press **Enter**, the computer will print as much as it can on the first line, depending on the size of your window, and continue on the next line:

```
>>> print("A gorilla's diet is mainly vegetarian.\
They feed mainly on stems, bamboo shoots and fruits.")
A gorilla's diet is mainly vegetarian.They feed mainly on st
ems, bamboo shoots and fruits.
>>>
```

Challenge 1

Write a Python statement to display the line:

```
Gorillas are the largest living primates.
```

Challenge 2

Write a Python **print** statement, split over two lines, to print the following output on one line. Use the tip above to help you:

```
The scientific name for the Western Lowland
gorilla is "Gorilla gorilla gorilla"
```

Splitting output over two lines

Example 4

Suppose you want to print a quotation, with the author's name (Steven Wright) on a separate line, like this :

```
"If at first you don't succeed, skydiving definitely isn't for you."
- Steven Wright
```

To print an output over two lines, you can use two **print** statements.

Alternatively, you can insert the **newline character \n**, which is equivalent to an **"Enter"** character.

```
>>> print('"If at first you don't succeed, \
skydiving definitely isn't for you."\n- Steven Wright')
"If at first you don't succeed, skydiving definitely isn't for you."
- Steven Wright
```

! Tip

If you enter something that Python cannot interpret, it will display an error message like this:

```
>>> prnt("Hello")
Traceback (most recent call last):
  File "<stdin>", line 1, in <module>
    prnt("Hello")
NameError: name 'prnt' is not defined
```

Challenge 3 📖

Write a single Python **print** statement to print "Don't worry. Be happy." on two separate lines.

The Editor window

So far, you have typed your statements in Python's Shell window. This is very useful for trying out new statements, but you can't save a program in this window.

In the Editor window of Python's **Integrated Development Environment (IDLE)**, you can write, save, edit and run your programs.

Starting a new program

Load Python and select *File, New File* in the Interactive window.

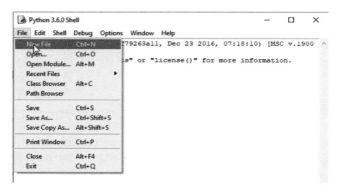

The Editor window will open.

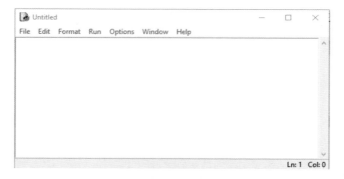

! **Tip**

You can open a new or existing file from the **File** menu in either the Python Shell (Interactive window) or the Editor window.

You can open the Python Shell (Interactive window) from the **Run** menu in the Editor window.

Create or select a suitable folder to save your programs. Type the short program shown below. Then select *File, Save* from the menu, or use the shortcut key combination **Ctrl-S**, and save it in your folder, naming the file **Greeting**. Run your program by clicking *Run, Run Module* from the menu, or by pressing the shortcut key **F5**.

The name of your file is shown here

The output will be displayed in the Interactive (Shell) window

! **Tip**

You can press the shortcut key F5 instead of selecting *Run, Run Module* to run your program

Syntax highlighting used in the code

IDLE uses different text shades to highlight different types of statement. This helps make the code more readable and can also help identify errors.

Red is used for comments in the program. Comments have no effect on the program, but they are very useful for giving information such as the name of a program, and what different parts of a longer program do.

Purple is used for Python reserved words or commands such as print, input.

Green is used for text in quotes.

Orange is used for keywords used in Python such as if, else, while

Black is used for variable names such as firstName, symbols such as +, −, *, / and other parts of the code.

Text output in the Shell window is displayed in blue.

Syntax errors

It is surprisingly hard to type even a few lines of code without a mistake. If you have made any errors when typing your code, you might see a message like this:

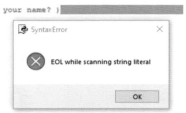

```
#Program name Challenge 5 Greeting (syntax error)

print("Hi there!\n")
firstName = input("What is your name? )
print("Hello", firstName)
```

SyntaxError ✕

✕ EOL while scanning string literal

OK

! Tip

If you see a **SyntaxError** message, it means you have written a statement incorrectly. The mistake is likely to be in the line highlighted, or it may be in the line above.

Comments

Python ignores any line or part of a line which starts with **#**. This identifies the text as a **comment**. Comments are very useful for giving information about the program, such as its name and purpose. They can be used anywhere in the code to explain a line or section of code.

Challenge 5 📖 📁

Copy the program above and spot the error in the code. If you have made an error in your program, click **OK** in the message box, correct the error, save the program by pressing **Ctrl-S**, and test it again by pressing **F5**.

Challenge 6 📁

Using the example shown in the screenshot above as a guide, write, save and run a program to ask the user to input the names of three animals.

Print the animal names out once all they have all been entered.

Include two comments to document the program name and describe what it does.

Tip: Use three `input` statements. You can use either one or three `print` statements.

Variables

A **variable** is like a storage container in memory that can hold information such as a number, a person's name or a whole sentence. You can replace the contents of the variable whenever you need.

To create a variable, decide what you want to call it and then put something into it using an = sign.

```
temperature = 28.5
country = "Italy"
a = 6
```

This is called "assigning a value to a variable".

Rules for variable names

- A variable name, or **identifier**, may only contain alpha-numeric characters (A–Z, a–z, 0–9) and underscores (_)
- A variable name must start with a letter (not a number) or the underscore character
- Variable names are case-sensitive. `gameScore`, `gamescore` and `GameScore` are three different variables.

! Tip

CamelCase is commonly used to separate words making up a variable name; for example, totalDistance, studentName, Variable names by convention start with a lowercase letter.

A variable is **assigned** a value using the = sign. These are examples of **assignment statements**:

```
speed = 560
gameEnded = True
password = "Frederika79#"
```

Challenge 7

Identify a variable used in your solution to Challenge 6.

Challenge 8

Identify and correct the syntax errors in the program below which is saved in the **Starred challenges (incomplete)** folder. Correct the errors, test the program and save it in your own folder. The corrected program is in the **Challenge solutions** folder.

```
#Program name: Challenge 8 Program with syntax errors
Correct the syntax errors in this program
print("This program contains syntax errors"\n)
favourite-animal = "Giraffe"
scariestAnimal = Lion
print("Favourite animal", favourite-animal, \n
      "Scariest animal...." scariestAnimal)
```

Constants

Some programming languages allow you to define constants, whose value, once defined, cannot be changed during execution of the program. You cannot declare a value as a constant in Python. Instead, a value that will never, or rarely change, for example **PI, SPEED_OF_LIGHT**, or **TAX_RATE** is commonly assigned an identifier all in uppercase letters.

Challenge 9

Which of the following are valid variable names?

(a) myBestScore

(b) Name

(c) 1stClass

(d) cost_of_meal

(e) print84

(f) A–1

(g) _1234

Challenge 10

Predict what is printed when Python runs these statements.

```
x = 5
y = 10
x = y
y = 5
print(x, y)
```

Challenge 11

Predict what is printed when Python runs these statements.

```
x = "Tom"
y = "Fred"
z = "Henry"
z = y
y = x
x = z
print(x, y, z)
```

Challenge 12

Type the statements in Challenges 10 and 11 into the Python Shell to verify your answers.

Input statements

When data needs to be input from a keyboard, a prompt is usually displayed telling the user to type something. Whatever they type is automatically assigned to a **string** variable specified by the user.

Example 5

The first statement displays a prompt, asking the user to input their name. It accepts a name, for example **Holly**, then displays **Hello Holly** on the screen.

```
firstName = input("Please enter your first name: ")
print("Hello", firstName)
```

The first statement displays on the screen

```
Please enter your name:
```

and waits for the user to enter something. If the user types **Holly**, the **print** statement then displays on the screen:

```
Hello Holly
```

The first statement could be written as two separate statements:

```
print("Please enter your name: ")
firstName = input()
```

It is generally more convenient to write one statement to display a prompt and accept user input.

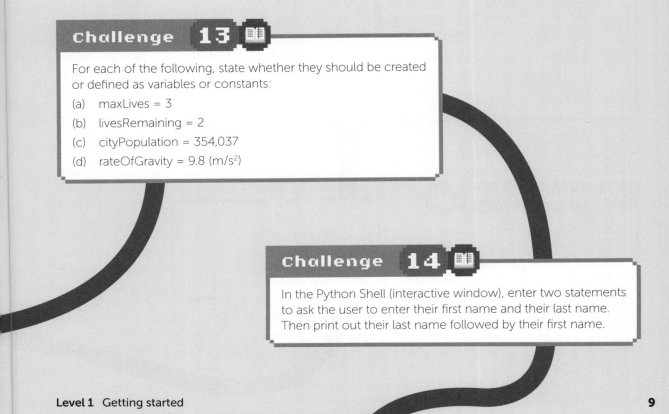

Challenge 13

For each of the following, state whether they should be created or defined as variables or constants:

(a) maxLives = 3

(b) livesRemaining = 2

(c) cityPopulation = 354,037

(d) rateOfGravity = 9.8 (m/s^2)

Challenge 14

In the Python Shell (interactive window), enter two statements to ask the user to enter their first name and their last name. Then print out their last name followed by their first name.

Concatenation

As well as being used for addition, the symbol + is also used to **concatenate**, or join together, two strings.

```
>>> "Ben" + " " + "Miller"
'Ben Miller'
```

Numbers enclosed in quotes, or input as strings, behave as strings, not numbers:

```
>>> "15" + "7"
'157'
```

Experiment with using a comma between strings and numbers instead of concatenating two strings with a + symbol:

```
>>> print("Ben", "Miller", 27)
Ben Miller 27
```

Challenge 15 ★ 📁

Load the incomplete program below which is saved in the **Python Programs\ Starred challenges (incomplete)** folder, or copy the statements as shown:

```
#Program name: Challenge 15 name and blood type incomplete
lastname = input("Please enter your last name: ")
initial = input("Please enter your initial: ")
bloodType = input("Enter your blood type: ")
```

Add a **print** statement to print, for example,

```
Name: Johnson F     Blood type: O negative
```

Save and run your program.

Challenge 16 📖

Debugging or error messages can seem a little cryptic at first. What might the following syntax error messages indicate?
(a) `EOL while scanning string literal`
(b) `NameError: name 'lastnamee' is not defined`

LEVEL 2
DATA TYPES AND OPERATORS

Data types

Different data types are held differently in a computer's memory, so you need to use the correct data type for the task. The table below shows the data types used in Python.

Data type	Type of data	Examples
Integer	A whole number	3, −170, 176500
Real/float	A number with a decimal point	3.142, 78.0, −0.5678
Char/ character	A single character – any letter, digit, punctuation mark or symbol that can be typed	A, #, @, 6, !
String	Zero or more characters enclosed in quote marks	"yes", "Hi John", ""
Boolean	Can only take the value True or False	True, False

Arithmetic operators

The standard arithmetic operators used by Python are shown below. The normal rules of precedence hold, i.e. parentheses (brackets), exponents, multiplication, division, addition, subtraction.

Operation	Operator	Python operator	Python example	Result
Addition	+	+	21 + 6	27
Subtraction	−	−	17 − 8	9
Multiplication	*	*	5 * 3	15
Division	/	/	13 / 4	3.25
Exponentiation	^	**	3**2	9
Integer division	div	//	19 // 5	3
Modulus (remainder)	mod	%	19 % 5	4

> **! Tip**
>
> Normal rules of precedence mean that in an expression such as:
> 3 + 5 * (6 + 10) / 2 ** 2
> the operations are carried out in the order: Parentheses (Brackets), Exponents (Order), Multiplication, Division, Addition, Subtraction. The answer to this expression is 23.0.

Integer division and finding a remainder

Sometimes you may want to perform **integer division** and find a **remainder**.

Example 1

Fifty vouchers for free rides at a fair are to be divided among 16 children. Calculate how many vouchers each child will receive and how many will be left over.

```
vouchersPerChild = 50 // 16
leftover = 50 % 16
```

Challenge 17 ★ 📁

Complete the program **Challenge 17 Divide books among children incomplete** in the **Python Programs\Starred challenges (incomplete)** folder. The program is designed to specify the total number of books available to be given to a group of children. It then calculates and prints how many books each child will receive and how many will be left over.

```
#Program name: Challenge 17 Divide books among children incomplete
books = 650
children = 173
booksPerChild = ...........................
booksLeftOver = .........................
#print number of books to be given to each child
print("Books per child: ",..................... )
#print number of books left over
.........................................
```

Note: You can check your program against the completed program in the
Python Programs\Challenge solutions folder.

Printing calculated results

You can carry out a calculation within the **print** statement.

Example 2

```
PI = 3.142
radius = 6
print("Area of circle: ", PI * radius ** 2)
```

Challenge 18

Complete the Python statement to print:

    "13685 divided by 27 = ... remainder ..... "

(Use the operators for calculating integer division and remainder)

Challenge 19

A personal pedometer tracks and records the distance walked each day by the wearer.

Choose meaningful names (identifiers) for two variables holding the number of miles walked on each day for two days, Monday and Tuesday. Assign values (each with a decimal point) to these variables.

Write a single statement to calculate and print the total miles walked, for example:

    Total miles walked on Monday and Tuesday = 43.75

Challenge 20

Write a statement to calculate and display the answer to the calculation:

    (7 * 3) + (16 / 5)

Challenge 21

Write a statement to calculate and print the result of 2^{10} in the format:

    2 to the power 10 = ...

An assignment statement always contains an = sign, but it is not an equation. It means
"Take whatever is on the right-hand side of the = sign and put it into the variable named on the
left-hand side of the = sign."

Simple assignment statements look like this:

```
age = 17
distanceTravelled = 35.6
street = "Granville Street"
over18 = False
winner = True
count = count + 1
```

The last statement adds 1 to whatever was in the variable **count** and puts the result back in **count**.

Challenge 22

Enter the following statements in the Python Shell (Interactive window).

```
cabFare = 4.50
flight = 91.25
train = 11.80
total = cabFare + flight + train
print("Total travel expenses =",total)
```

This should print:

```
Total travel expenses = 107.55
```

Converting from strings to numbers

In Python, all data items input by the user are treated as **string** variables. Numbers input by the user have to be converted to either integers or floating point numbers before they can be used in calculations.

Function	Description	Example	Returns
float(x)	Converts a string to a floating point value	float("4.65")	4.65
int(x)	Converts a string to an integer	int("3")	3
str(x)	Converts a number x to a string value	str(5.0)	'5.0'

To convert a string to an integer, use the `int()` function.
To convert a string to a floating point number, use the `float()` function.

Inputting numerical data

Example 3

```
#Program name: Level 2 Example 3 Add and multiply two integers
x = int(input("Enter the first integer: "))
y = int(input("Enter the second integer: "))
sumXY = x + y
product = x * y
print("Sum =", sumXY)
print("Product =", product)
```

Example 4

Below is a Python program to allow the user to enter costs of travel, using the same values as in Challenge 22. The statements appear as follows:

```
#Program name: Level 2 Example 4 Cost of travel
cabFare = input("Enter cost of the cab fare: ")
flight = input("Enter cost of your flight: ")
train = input("Enter cost of any train fare: ")
total = cabFare + flight + train
print("Total travel expenses: ",total)
```

Run and test the program using 4.50, 91.25 and 11.80 as input values. The output appears as:

```
Total travel expenses: 4.5091.2511.80
```

What has happened? All the data has been entered as strings and concatenated (joined together) in the `print` statement. All the costs need to be converted to floating point values.

Challenge 23

Amend the program shown in Example 4 so that it gives the correct total cost.

! Tip

Changing the type of a variable is called **"casting"**.

Challenge 24

For each of the following variables, state whether they need to be of **string**, **integer** or **float** type.

(a) numberOfSiblings

(b) name

(c) price

Challenge 25

Write statements to ask a truck driver to enter the weight of their goods in pounds (lb), convert the data to an integer and add 24,350 lbs to it to adjust for the weight of the truck. Print out the combined (laden) weight, e.g.

    The laden weight of the truck is .... lbs.

Convert the weight to kilos and output the result as an integer. There are 2.2 lbs to a kg.

Challenge 26

A taxi company charges a basic fee of $4.00 plus $0.80 per km. To estimate the cost of a taxi fare, the cab driver inputs the number of km from the airport to a hotel, and the computer calculates and outputs the fare.

Write a Python program to do this.

Challenge 27

The formula for converting a Fahrenheit temperature (F) to Celsius (C) is

$$C = (F - 32) * 5 / 9$$

Write a program to allow a user to enter a Fahrenheit temperature, convert the temperature to Celsius and print out the result of the conversion.

Test your program four times, entering temperatures of 212, 89.5, 32, −40

At what temperature are the Fahrenheit and Celsius temperatures the same value?

Using concatenation in input and output statements

When writing an **input** statement, sometimes you need to include a variable in the prompt. You can do this by concatenating the different parts of the prompt.

Example 5

```
day = input("Please enter the day of the week: ")
hours = float(input("How many hours did you walk for on " + day + "? "))
print("You walked " + str(hours) + " hours on " + day)
```

> **! Tip**
>
> Remember, you can only concatenate strings. If you want to concatenate a string and an integer, convert the integer to a string first.

Challenge 28

Assign values to two integer variables **num1** and **num2**. Write a single **print** statement to add the two numbers and print, for example, **The sum of 24 and 3 is 27**. Test your answer in the Python Shell window

Challenge 29

Write a program to accept the name of a student, e.g. Ron. Then write an **input** statement which displays the prompt:

"Enter mark out of 20 scored by Ron: ".

In the **print** statement, multiply the mark by 5 to display the mark as a percentage, e.g.

Ron scored 75 percent

Challenge 30 📖

Write statements to accept from the user, values for two variables named x and y. Then swap the contents of x and y, and print their new values.

Challenge 31 ⭐ 📁

A cyclist training for a race records his times over 35 miles for two consecutive days. His times are 2 hours 58 minutes and 3 hours 10 minutes.

Complete the Python program **Challenge 15 average cyclist time incomplete** in the **Starred challenges (incomplete)** folder to calculate his average time in minutes. Convert the average to hours and minutes and print the result.

Challenge 32 📁

Write a program to ask a rocket launch controller to input a number of hours as an integer between 50 and 100. Convert this to days and hours and print the results in the format:

```
Launch in xx days, xx hours.
```

Challenge 33 📖

Enter statements

```
num = 16
num = num + 1
num = num + 3
print("num", num)
```

What is printed?

LEVEL 3
SELECTION

A number of statements that are executed one after the other in the order they appear in a program is a programming construct called a **sequence**. In the next two levels two other basic constructs, called **selection** and **iteration** will be covered.

Comparison and logical operators

Operators fall into two categories:

- **comparison** (or **relational**) operators such as **> (greater than)**, **== (equal)** and **!= (not equal)**
- **logical** operators include **and**, **or**, and, **not**. Logical operators are also known as **Boolean operators**.

The table shows all the comparison and logical operators.

Operation name	Python operator
Less than	<
Greater than	>
Less than or equal	<=
Greater than or equal	>=
Equal	==
Not equal	!=
Logical and	and
Logical or	or
Logical not	not

A **Boolean data type** can be either **True** or **False**.

A **Boolean expression** involves a comparison or logical operator such as

```
height > 2000
temperature <= 0
```

and results in either **True** or **False**.

19

Example 1

In the Python interactive window, type each of the statements below shown next to the >>> prompt. You will see the output shown in blue.

```
>>> 16 > 16.5
False
>>> 27 == 9 * 3
True
>>> (7 > 4) and (2 <= 2)
True
>>> print(23 % 7 < 23 // 7)
True
```

Challenge 34

In the Python Shell, code a Boolean expression equivalent to the statement:

10 times 7 is equal to 70

Press **Enter** to display the result.

Challenge 35

In the Python Shell, code a Boolean expression equivalent to:

"John" is not equal to "JOHN"

Press **Enter** to display the result.

Challenge 36

In the Python Shell, code a Boolean expression equivalent to:

6 is less than or equal 2*4 and 28 is less than or equal 7*4

Press **Enter** to display the result.

Challenge 37

Write a Boolean expression equivalent to "Both x and y are negative"

Challenge 38

Write a Boolean expression equivalent to "Either a or b is zero"

Challenge 39 📖

What is printed when the following statements are executed?

```
a = 24 / 8
b = 24 + 8
print(a == b)
```

Copy the statements into the Python Shell to verify your answer.

Challenge 40 📖

In the Python Shell, write a statement which evaluates and prints a Boolean expression equivalent to:

237 // 17 is equal to 237 / 17

Challenge 41 📖

What is printed when the following statement is executed?

```
print((10 == 5 * 2) and (45 != 9 * 5))
```

Copy the statements into the Python Shell to verify your answer.

Challenge 42 📖

What is printed when the following statement is executed?

```
print((6 * 3 >= 9 * 2) or (30 // 7 == 2))
```

Copy the statements into the Python Shell to verify your answer.

Selection statements

Selection statements such as `if`, or `if .. else` are used together with a Boolean expression to control which instruction is executed next.

Example 2

A child is permitted to ride on the Twister only if they are 10 years old or over.

```
age = int(input("Enter age: "))
if age < 10:
   print("Sorry, you are too young for this ride! ")
```

Example 3

The `if … else` statement below specifies what should happen if the Boolean condition evaluates to **False**.

```
age = int(input("Enter age: "))
if age < 10:
   print("Sorry, you are too young for this ride! ")
else:
   print("Continue through gate. ")
```

Indentation

Indenting your code is essential in Python. It shows where a block of code begins and ends. This makes the program easier to follow and easier to debug.

The Python editor will automatically indent your code for you – be careful if you need to change this.

Challenge 43

Write a program to input the left- and right-hand weights of a rollercoaster ride car. If the two weights are equal, print "The car is balanced". If the weights are not equal, print "The car is not balanced." Include at least two comments in your program.

Save the program as **Challenge 43 Ride car balance** and test it with different weights.

Compare your answer with the program in the **Python programs\Challenge solutions** folder.

Challenge 44

Complete the program below to check tyre pressure. If it is between 28 PSI and 32 PSI, print "Tyre pressure OK". Otherwise, print "Tyre pressure too high or too low".

```
pressure = int(input("Input tyre pressure in PSI: "))
if .............................................
    ...................................
etc.
```

! Tip

Brackets are optional in the `if` statement but make the statement clearer.

Challenge 45

Write a program to input the length and width of a maze. If the two sides are equal, print "The maze is square". If the sides are not equal, print "The maze is rectangular." Include at least two comments in your program.

Save the program as **Challenge 45 Maze dimensions**, and test it with different maze dimensions.

Compare your answer with the program in the **Python programs\Challenge solutions** folder.

The if..elif..else statement

'Elif' stands for 'else if'. You can test several different conditions using the `if..elif..else` statement.

Example 4

The program below inputs the current battery charge on a mobile phone. If it is below 20%, it prints "Low battery. Charge required.". If it is between 21% and 99%, it prints "Battery charge OK.". If it is 100%, it prints "Fully charged.".

```
#Program name: Level 3 Example 4 Mobile battery
charge = int(input("Input battery charge %: "))
if charge <= 20:
    print("Low battery. Charge required.")
elif charge == 100:
    print("Fully charged.")
else:
    print("Battery charge OK.")
```

Challenge 46 ★

Complete the program **Challenge 46 Quiz incomplete**, saved in the **Starred challenges (incomplete)** folder. The program asks three quiz questions and scores the answers, giving the total score at the end.

Nested selection statements

If there is more than one condition to be tested after the initial choice of options is made, you can use two **if** statements, one nested inside the other.

Example 5

The program below calculates the entrance charge to a water park.

During the week, junior members pay €1.00 and senior members pay €2.00. At weekends, junior members pay €2.00 and senior members pay €5.00.

For simplicity, no validation of user entry is carried out in this program – you could assume that data entry is made in real life by pressing the correct buttons on a special data entry pad.

```
#Program name: Level 3 Example 5 water park entry fee
#Program calculates entrance fee

weekendRate = input("Weekend Rate? (Enter Y or N): ")
visitor = input("Enter J for Junior, S for Senior): ")
if weekendRate == "Y":
    if visitor == "J":
        entryFee = 2.00
    else:
        entryFee = 5.00
else:
    if visitor == "J":
        entryFee = 1.00
    else:
        entryFee = 2.00

print("Entry Fee: ", entryFee)
```

Challenge 47

Write a program to measure a user's resting heart rate.

Ask the user: "Have you been at rest for at least 20 minutes?"

If the user inputs "Y", ask the user "Is your pulse rate between 60 and 100 bpm?"

If their pulse is between 60 and 100 bpm, print "Your heart rate is within the expected range." otherwise print "Your resting heart rate is outside of the expected range. You may wish to seek further advice from a professional."

If the user inputs "N", print "Rest for 20 minutes and try again!"

Challenge 48 ★ 🗀

An airport ATM (cash machine) has a Fast Cash option which allows a user to select a withdrawal amount of £20, £50 or £100. Load the incomplete program named **Challenge 48 Fast cash incomplete**, which simulates some of the available options, from the **Starred challenges (incomplete)** folder.

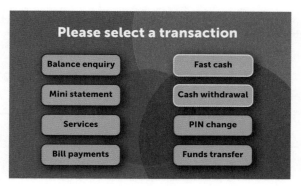

Remember:
You can cancel a running program any time by pressing Ctrl-C in the Python Shell window.

Complete the program. Run the completed program and test all the options.

- What happens if you enter 4 for the transaction number?
- What happens if you enter an amount of 200 instead of 20, 50 or 100?
- How many times will you need to run the program to test all the different options?

The completed program is in the **Challenge solutions** folder.

Testing a program

After you have written a program and got it running, you should test it thoroughly using a test plan. You need to create a test plan that includes:

- **Invalid data**. For example, a non-numeric character input when a numeric value is expected.
- **Boundary data**, and data on either side of a boundary. For example, if an input value must be greater than 17, test with input 16, 17 and 18.
- **Valid data** in the range of allowable values.

Challenge 49 ★ 🗀

Civil defence sirens are used around the world in case of emergency (for example tornados, tsunamis) or to call a local volunteer fire service to action. A manufacturer tests each of three models of siren for use before they leave the factory. Complete the program **Challenge 49 Siren decibels incomplete**, saved in the **Starred challenges (incomplete)** folder. The program determines whether a recorded level of decibels meets the acceptable minimum requirement for each of three models produced.

Use the following test data to test your program. (Challenge 49.)

Test	Model	dB level	Expected result	Actual result
1	A	93	"Failed minimum limit"	
2	B	110	"Failed. Requires adjustment or reclassification as Model A"	
3	C	110	"Failed. Requires adjustment or reclassification"	
4	C	126	"Passed"	
5				
6				
7				

Make up three more tests to test different aspects of the program. Your tests should include valid and invalid data, boundary data and normal data.

LEVEL 4
ITERATION

Iteration means repetition. Computers are very good at repeating the same instruction hundreds or thousands of times, using different data.

The *for* loop

This type of loop is used when you know how many times the instructions are to be repeated. This is known as **definite iteration**.

Note: The range (2,11) means that the range starts at 2 but ends at 10, not 11. Programs for Examples 1–4 are given in **Level 4 Examples 1–4 different ranges in FOR loops** in the **Examples folder**.

Example 1

```
for count in range(2,11):
    n = count * 7
    print(count, "x 7 =",n)
```

This will print:

```
2 X 7 = 14
3 X 7 = 21
..................... to
10 X 7 = 70
```

Example 2

If the range starts at 0, you can write, for example:

```
for j in range(5):
    jsquared = j * j
    print(j, jsquared)
```

This will print numbers and their squares from 0 to 4.

Example 3

You can specify the step by which the count is to be increased each time round the loop:

To print every 7th number between 7 and 35:

```
for n in range(0,36,7):
    print(n)
```

This will print the numbers 7, 14, 21, 28, 35

Example 4

You can specify a negative step:

To print every 7th number between 35 and 7 in descending order:

```
for n in range(35,6,-7):
    print(n)
```

This will print the numbers 35, 28, 21, 14, 7

> **Tip**
>
> Loop control variables are commonly called `count`, `i`, `j` or `n`.

Challenge 52

Write a program for an arcade game to display "You win!" three times and then print "Congratulations!".

Challenge 53

Write a program to count down from 10 to 0, displaying each value on a separate line.

Challenge 54

Write a program to ask the user which times table they would like to see displayed. Display the table from 2 to 12.

Challenge 55

Write a program to ask the user to input two positive integers **a** and **b** where a < b. Print all the numbers between **a** and **b** inclusive that are divisible by 13.

Challenge 56

Write a test plan for Challenge 55 to include test data for different user entries, together with expected results. Test your program.

Challenge 57

Write a program to count numbers from 0 to 100 in 5s and print them all on one line.

Tip: include the parameter `end = ""` in the print statement. e.g. `print(n, end = "")` to prevent going to a new line after executing a `print` statement.

Challenge 58

Write a program that asks an employee to enter their overtime hours each day of the week to the nearest quarter hour, e.g. 1.25. The total overtime over the week is calculated and printed at the end of the program.

Challenge 59

Write a program that asks a user to enter 5 numbers with decimal points between 1.0 and 10.0. Print out how many of the numbers entered are whole numbers.

Tip: Use the functions `float(x)` and `int(x)`.

Nested *for* loop

One loop can be nested inside another.

Example 5

The program below prints stars to form a triangle.

```
#Program name: Level 4 Example 5 triangle of stars
for row in range(1,11):
    for column in range(row):
        print("*", end = "")
    print() #go to a new line
```

```
*
**
***
****
*****
******
*******
********
*********
**********
```

Challenge 60

Write a program to display the times tables 7 to 10, displaying each table in the format

```
7 x 1 = 7
7 x 2 = 14
etc.
```

Challenge 61

A store sells a brand of Italian bathroom tiles in different lengths and widths. Tiles come in lengths of 10, 15, 20cm and in widths of 10 and 12cm, or in lengths of 4, 6 and 8 inches and in widths of 4 and 5 inches. Customers can select which units to use.

Write a program to ask the user to choose their preferred units of measurement and then calculate and print, for each length and each width, the area covered by one tile.

The *while* loop

A `while` loop is useful when you want the instructions in a loop to be executed repeatedly until a certain condition is met. It is an example of **indefinite iteration**.

Example 6

The user enters the number of lengths of a pool they swam over several days. An entry of –1 signals that there is no more data to enter. The total number of lengths and the daily average is calculated.

```
#Program Level 4 Example 6 Average number of lengths swum v1

day = 0
totalLengths = 0
lengths = int(input("Enter number of lengths: "))

while lengths != -1:
    day = day + 1
    totalLengths = totalLengths + lengths
    lengths = int(input("Enter number of lengths, -1 to end: "))

averageLengths = totalLengths / day
print("Average daily number of lengths:", averageLengths)
```

The program is tested with input values 3, 4, 4, –1.

This produces output:

```
Enter number of lengths: 3
Enter number of lengths: 4
Enter number of lengths: 4
Enter number of lengths: -1
Average daily number of lengths: 3.6666666666666665
```

In the above example, the **while** loop condition is tested **before** any of the instructions within the loop are performed. A common technique is to have the first **input** statement **outside** the loop, and have an **input** statement as the last instruction within the loop. The end-of-data test: (`lengths != -1`) will then be done before the first instruction in the loop is performed and therefore the next instruction to be executed will be:

```
averageLengths = totalLengths / day
```

Challenge 62

Write a program to ask the user to enter the number of lengths swum by Jane on a certain day. If the number of lengths is not between 10 and 150, ask the user to re-enter until a valid length is entered. Print a short message "Data accepted" when valid data is entered.

The round() function

The **round()** function rounds a floating point variable to the specified number of decimal places.

Example 7

```
x = 6.548784
print(round(x, 2)) #will print 6.55
```

An alternative solution to Example 6

There are usually many different ways of writing a program that will all produce correct results.

We can make the program shown in Example 6 more user-friendly with a more informative message for data entry. In the version below, only one **input** statement is used. An **if** statement is used to check whether −1 has been entered.

The prompt in the **input** statement uses **concatenation** (see page 17). It also uses **casting** (see Page 16) to convert the integer result of **day + 1** to a string.

Example 8

```
#Program Level 4 Example 8 Average number of lengths swum v2

day = 0
totalLengths = 0
moreData = True
print("Enter -1 when no more data")
while moreData:
    lengths = int(input("Enter number of lengths on day "\
      + str(day + 1) + ": "))
    if lengths != -1:
        day = day + 1
        totalLengths = totalLengths + lengths
    else:
        moreData = False

averageLengths = totalLengths / day
print("Average daily number of lengths:", round(averageLengths, 1))
```

Challenge 63

Enter the program in Example 6, using the same test data. Use the **round()** function to round **averageLengths** to 1 decimal place. Save and execute your program.

Challenge 64

Enter, save and run the program in Example 8. What does the prompt say now?

Challenge 65

Write a program to enter the names and times in seconds of runners participating in 100m race heats. The program should prompt for a name, then prompt for their time, e.g.

Enter time in seconds for King, R:

The end of data is signalled by entering **xxx** for the runner's name.

Print the average time, in seconds, of all the runners.

Challenge 66 ★

Load **Challenge 66 Tiles required to cover given area incomplete** from the **Starred challenges (incomplete)** folder.

The program asks the user to enter the size in m² of an area that needs tiling. The user then selects the size of tiles they want from a range of sizes given in cm. The program tells them how many tiles they will need. (Ten percent is added to the calculated number to allow for tiles that need to be cut, and this number is rounded down to the nearest whole number.)

Copy and complete the program and save it in your own folder.

Test your completed program by entering 20 cm for tile length, 12 cm for tile width and 2.4 m² for area to be covered. The integer number of tiles required, including the 10% extra), is 110.

Challenge 67 ★

Load **Challenge 67 Double a number repeatedly incomplete** from the **Starred challenges (incomplete)** folder.

The program asks the user to enter a number between 1 and 10. If the number is not in this range, keep printing a warning message and asking the user to re-enter the number. Then keep doubling this number until the result is 100,000 or more. Print the final result and the number of times the number was doubled.

Challenge 68

Amend the program **Challenge 68 Double a number repeatedly completed** so that the user can enter the final target. Include validation to ensure the target entered by the user is between 20 and 100,000. Also include a **print** statement so that the number, and number of times doubled, is printed each time it is doubled.

Finding the maximum or minimum of a set of data

Sometimes you may need to find the maximum or minimum of a set of values entered by the user.

If you are asked to find the minimum of a set of values, start by setting an initial value larger than the maximum possible value. For example if you were asked to find the minimum (fastest) time achieved by a number of swimmers during competition heats over 100 metres, you could set a variable called `minTime` to 1000 seconds. Every time a user inputs a time less than `minTime`, you replace `minTime` with the new value.

Example 9

The following program finds and prints the name and time in seconds achieved over 100 metres by the fastest swimmer in a competition.

```
#Program name: Level 4 Example 9 Fastest swimmer name and time

totalTime = 0
minTime = 1000
moreData = True
while moreData:
    name = input("Enter name of swimmer: ")
    if name != "xxx":
        swimTime = float(input("Enter time in seconds for " + name + ": "))
        if swimTime < minTime:
            minTime = swimTime
            fastestSwimmer = name
    else:
        moreData = False

print("Fastest swimmer:", fastestSwimmer)
print("Time:", minTime, "seconds")
```

> **! Tip**
>
> Remember:
> You can cancel a running program any time by pressing Ctrl-C in the Python Shell window.

Challenge 69

Enter the names and scores out of 10 (e.g. 7.5) achieved by divers in a competition. The end of data is indicated by a name of **xxx**. Print the name and score of the diver with the best score, and the average of all the scores, rounded to 1 decimal place. (Assume there are no ties for first place.)

Challenge 70

Write a program to:

- allow a user to enter the names and years of five Olympic Games cities.
- calculate and print the names and years of the two cities with the most recent and earliest years.

ARRAYS AND LISTS

An **array** is a data structure that stores values of the same data type, such as integers, floating point numbers, characters or strings.

An array is a common data structure in languages such as Visual Basic and Java, but a **list** is a much more common data structure in Python. In Python, a list is used instead of an array.

A Python **list** can store values of different data types, for example:

```
list1 = ["Alan", "Johnson", 27, "M", "Blonde"]
```

Working with lists

You can print the contents of a list with a single **print** statement.

Try this in the Python Shell:

```
>>> list1 = ["Alan", "Johnson", 27, "M", "Blonde"]
>>> print(list1)
['Alan', 'Johnson', 27, 'M', 'Blonde']
```

Initialising a variable or a list provides a starting value. You can initialise a list like this:

```
planet = ["Jupiter", "Saturn", "Uranus", "Neptune", "Earth", "Venus"]
```

Items in a list may be referred to using an **index**. The first item has an index of 0.

```
print(planet[0]) #will print Jupiter
```

Example 1

Print all the items in the **planet** list, with each item on a separate line.

```
#Program name: Level 5 Example 1 List of planets

planet = ["Mercury", "Venus", "Earth", "Mars", "Jupiter", "Saturn"]
n = len(planet) #sets n equal to number of items in the list
for index in range(n):
    print(planet[index])
```

Challenge 71 📖 📁

Write a single statement to print the list of planets.

List methods and functions

(See Page 45 for comparison of methods and functions.)

Method / Function	Description	Example
`list.append(item)`	Adds a new item to the end of the list	`planet.append("Uranus")`
`del <list>[<index>]`	Removes the item at index from the list	`del planet[3]`
`list.insert(index,item)`	Inserts an item just before an existing one at index	`planet.insert(3,"Pluto")`
`<item> = list()` `<item> = []`	Two methods of creating an empty list structure	`planet = list()` `planet = []`

Challenge 72

Write a program to initialise the list of planets:

`planet = ["Mercury", "Venus", "Earth", "Mars", "Jupiter", "Saturn"]`

Use the `list.append()` method to append Uranus and Neptune to the end of list.

Print the list in the format:

`['Mercury', 'Venus', 'Earth', 'Mars', 'Jupiter', 'Saturn', 'Uranus', 'Neptune']`

Challenge 73

Write a program to initialise the list:

`["Mercury", "Venus", "Mars", "Jupiter", "Saturn"]`

Use a list method to insert "Earth" between "Venus" and "Mars".
Print the amended list.

Challenge 74

Write a program to initialise and print the list of planets:

`planet = ["Mercury", "Venus", "Earth", "Mars", "Jupiter", "Saturn"]`

Then print the list with each planet on a separate line starting with Saturn, and ending with Mercury.

Challenge 75

Write a program to ask the user to enter the number of astronauts sent on space missions in the years 2016 to 2020. e.g. "How many astronauts on space missions in 2016?"

Store the numbers in a list named **astronauts**.

Print the list and the total number of astronauts sent on space missions from 2016 to 2020

> **! Tip**
>
> You can initialise a list named, for example, `myList` containing seven zeros using either of the two statements:
>
>   myList = [0]*7
> or
>   myList = [0,0,0,0,0,0,0]

Challenge 76

Write a statement to initialise a list named **totals** containing 100 zeros.

Challenge 77

Load the program **Challenge 77 Lists planet and moons with errors** from the folder, correct the syntax errors and find the logic error(s) by testing the program until it works correctly.

The program is intended to:

- create two empty lists named **planetList** and **moonList**.
- use a **while** loop to ask the user to enter the name of a planet and the number of moons it has, until there is no more data to be entered, indicated by an entry of **xxx**.
- append each name to the list **planetList**, and the number of moons to the list **moonList**.
- use a **for … next** loop to print the data from the lists, in the format

  `Mars has 2 moons.`
  `Earth has 1 moon`
  etc.

The following data is used to test the program:

Mars, 2
Earth, 1
Jupiter, 79

Challenge 78

Create two lists. One list contains the names of eight planets. The second list contains the sizes of the planets in percentages relative to earth.

> Jupiter 1120% the size of Earth
> Saturn 945% the size of Earth
> Uranus 400% the size of Earth
> Neptune 390% the size of Earth
> Venus 95% the size of Earth
> Mars 53% the size of Earth
> Mercury 38% the size of Earth
> Earth 100% the size of Earth

From the two lists, print the information in the format given above.

Challenge 79

Open the file **Challenge 79 Delete item from list of planets** from the **Starred challenges (incomplete)** folder. Complete the program to locate and delete the name **"Earth"** from the following list of planets.

```
planet = ["Mercury", "Venus", "Earth", "Mars", "Jupiter", "Saturn"]
```

Print the new list.

Challenge 80

Write a Python program to initialise and print the lists described in Challenge 78 and to amend the value for Neptune in the list given in Challenge 78. It should be 388%. Print the original lists and print the amended value, e.g. **Neptune 388%**.

Challenge 81

Write a program which prints the names of the largest and the smallest planets in the lists described in Challenge 78.

Two-dimensional lists

A two-dimensional list can be thought of as a table with rows and columns.

Example 2

The table below represents the number of people booking campervans owned by a campervan rental company at three separate sites between May and August.

	May	June	July	August
Cambridge	57	68	100	124
Newcastle	43	52	92	101
Manchester	72	78	84	90

The list could be initialised with the statement:

```
booking = [[57,68,100,124], [43,52,92,101], [72,78,84,90]]
```

The number of campervans booked in Cambridge in May is referred to as **booking[0][0]**

The number of campervans booked in Newcastle in July is referred to as **booking[1][2]**

To print the two-dimensional list:

```
print(booking)
```

This will print:

```
[[57, 68, 100, 124], [43, 52, 92, 101], [72, 78, 84, 90]]
```

To find the total number of campervans booked in May, add up the numbers in the first column:

```
totalMay = 0
for row in range(3):
    totalMay = totalMay + booking[row][0]
print("Total bookings in May: ",totalMay)
```

Example 3

To find the total number of campervans booked between May and August, you need a nested **for** loop:

```python
total = 0
for row in range(3):
    for column in range(4):
        total = total + booking[row][column]
print("Total bookings May - August: ",total)
```

Challenge 82

In Example 2, the figure for Newcastle in July has been incorrectly entered. Write a statement to amend the figure in the two-dimensional list **booking** to **96**.

Challenge 83

Write a program to ask the user which site and which month they would like to have the bookings displayed for, and display the figure.

Example 4

The caravan rental company wants to print the average number of bookings for each branch for the 4-month period, and the total overall bookings. Results should be displayed in the format:

```
Average booking for Cambridge: nnn.n
Average booking for Newcastle: nnn.n
Average booking for Manchester: nnn.n

Total bookings for all sites: nnn

#Program name: Level 5 Example 4 average bookings

booking = [ [ 1, 2, 3, 4],   #total 10
            [10,20,30,40],   #total 100
            [ 2, 3, 4, 5] ] #total 14
siteName = ["Cambridge", "Newcastle", "Manchester"]

#define empty lists
siteBookings = [0]*3
averageBookings = [0]*3
totalBookings = 0

#find total and average of each row
for site in range(3):
   for month in range(4):
      siteBookings[site] = siteBookings[site] + booking[site][month]
   totalBookings = totalBookings + siteBookings[site]
   averageBookings[site] = siteBookings[site] / 4

#print average bookings for each site over 4-month period
for site in range(3):
   print("Average booking in", siteName[site], "=" , \
      round(averageBookings[site],1))
print("\nTotal bookings at all sites: ",totalBookings)
```

Challenge 84

A new campervan site near Birmingham opened in August. Initialise the list as above with an extra row of zeros. Ask the user to enter the booking figure for August and save it in the amended two-dimensional list. Print the amended list.

! Tip

Use simple values for test data, such as those used above, so that you can easily calculate expected results.

Performers in a figure-skating competition are judged by three different judges. Each judge awards the skaters a score of between 0 and 100.

The scores are held in a two-dimensional list.

	Judge1	Judge2	Judge3
Amber	75	59	63
Cindy	88	91	94
Valentina	78	81	84
Isabella	65	69	73
Terri	90	84	69

Complete the program **Challenge 85 Figure skating competition incomplete** which calculates the total score of each skater and prints the name and score of the winner.

Complete the program **Challenge 86 Lion cubs incomplete**. The number of cubs born to three lionesses named Tatiana, Sabrina and Luna in two consecutive years, 2019 and 2020, is entered and the total number of cubs calculated and printed.

STRINGS

A sequence of characters enclosed in either single quotes or double quotes is referred to in Python as a **string**.

A string can be any length and can include

- letters and numbers
- whitespace, symbols such as !, &, %
- "escape" characters such as \n (newline)

The function **len(string)** returns the length of a string.

For example:

```
print(len("The long grass whispers"))
```

will print 23

Indexing strings

Characters in a string can be indexed in the same way as items in a Python list. The first character in the string **myString** is referred to as **myString[0]**.

Iterating through a string

You can examine each character in a string, one at a time:

```
myName = "Stuart"
for nchar in myname:
    print(nchar)
```

Challenge 87

In the Python Shell (Interactive window) type

```
numChars = len("5 Oak Street Anytown")
print(numChars)
```

What is printed?

Challenge 88

In the Python Shell type

```
print(len("Mary\nJo"))
```

What is printed? What do you deduce from this?

Challenge 90

Write a program to ask the user to enter a sentence. Calculate and print the number of times the letter "e" appears in the sentence.

Challenge 89

In the Python Shell, write Python statements to ask the user to enter their full name.

Print the total number of characters in the name, and the first and last characters.

String methods

There are many string methods which you may find useful. In this list, the examples use a string variable named `str`, which has been assigned the value `"Paul and Ava set off on a long journey."`

Method	Description	Example
find(<string>)	Returns the location of <string> in the original. Returns –1, if not found	`n = str.find("Ava")` returns n = 9 `n = str.find("Anna")` returns n = –1
index(<string>)	Returns the location of <string> in the original. Raises an exception if not found	`n = str.index("Ava")` returns n = 9 `n = str.index("Anna")` causes a runtime error, `"substring not found"`
isalpha()	Returns True, if all characters are alphabetic (a–z)	`allChars = str.isalpha()` assigns **False** to **allChars** (space is not an alphabetic character)
isalnum()	Returns True, if all characters are alphabetic (a–z) and digits (0–9)	`x = "abc123".isalnum()` returns `x = True`
isdigit()	Returns True, if all characters are digits (0–9), exponents are digits	`x = "51.9".isdigit()` returns `x = False`
isnumeric()	Returns True, if all characters are numeric (0–9), exponents and fractions are numeric	`x = "5176".isnumeric()` returns `x = True`
replace(s1,s2)	Returns original string with all occurrences of s1 replaced with s2	`str2 = str.replace("Paul","Vic")` returns `"Vic and Ava set off... etc "`

split(<char>)	Returns a list of all substrings in the original, using <char> as the separator	`strList = str.split(" ")`
		returns
		`['Paul', 'and', 'Ava', 'set', 'off', 'on', 'a', 'long', 'journey.']`

strip(<char>)	Returns original string with all occurrences of 'char' removed from front and back	`newstring = str.strip(".")` returns `"Paul and Ava set off on a long journey"`

upper()	Returns the original string in upper case	`newstring = str.upper()`
		returns
		`"PAUL AND AVA SET OFF ON A LONG JOURNEY."`

lower()	Returns the original string in lower case	`newstring = "ABCDE".lower()` returns `"abcde"`
isupper()	Returns True, if all characters are upper case	`allcaps = "ABCDE".isupper()` assigns **True** to **allcaps**
islower()	Returns True, if all characters are lower case	`allcaps = "ABcde".islower()` assigns **False** to **allcaps**

Methods and functions

A Python method is like a function, except that it is attached to an object. A statement calling a method is written differently from a statement calling a function.

A typical statement using the function `int(x)` is written:

```
age = int("36")                    #returns the integer 36
```

A typical statement using the method `lower()` is written:

```
userName = "JSmith".lower()    #returns "jsmith"
```

Example 1

```
#This program demonstrates some string methods
myString = "A cow has four stomachs. An octopus has three hearts."
myStringUppercase = myString.upper()
mystringLowercase = myString.lower()
print(myStringUppercase)
print(mystringLowercase)
```

Challenge 91

Copy and save the above program. Add further statements to print the results of using string methods `isalpha()`, `myString.split(" ")`, `myString.index()`, `mystring.replace(s1,s2)`

Challenge 92

Complete the program to assign the following text to a string variable **notice**:

"All coast bound trains will now depart from Platform 4. Passengers should wait on Platform 4."

Use a string method to replace both occurrences of "4" with "2A" and print the resulting sentence.

```
#Program name: Challenge 92 String replacement
#This program replaces all occurrences of "Platform 4" with "Platform 2A"
in a string

notice = "All coast bound trains will now depart from Platform 4.\n\
Passengers should wait on Platform 4."

newNotice = ...........................

......................................
```

Slicing strings

To isolate part of a string, you can use **slicing**. Using slicing you can isolate, for example, the third and fourth characters in a vehicle licence plate, the area code of a long telephone number or a section of a product code.

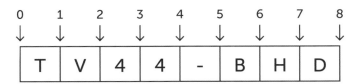

Example 2

The program below prints the first four and last three characters of a product code.

```
#Program name: Level 6 Example 2 Slicing strings
#This program shows how to isolate parts of a string

productCode = "TV44-BHD"

#isolate first 4 characters
chars1to4 = productCode [0:4]
print("First four characters are " + chars1to4)

#Find length of product code
n = len(productCode)
print("Length of product code:" , n)

#isolate last 3 characters
last3chars = productCode[n-3:n]
print("Last three characters are:", last3chars)
```

Load the program **Challenge 93 Product numbers incomplete** from the **Starred challenges (incomplete)** folder.

Complete this program to assign six product codes for televisions in the format **mmss xxx** (where **mm** represents the manufacturer and **ss** represents the size) to the list variable **productCode**, and print out all those with third and fourth digits equal to 32".

```
#Program name: Challenge 93 Product numbers incomplete
#This program processes a list of product numbers for televisions,
#printing all those with third and fourth digits equal to 32"

productCode = ["SN44-SHD","PS32-POR","HT60-BFS","SN32-UHD",
              "SG32-SMT","SN55-4KS"]
for index in range ...............
    .........................................
        .........................................
```

Load the program **Challenge 94 Book title incomplete** from the **Starred challenges (incomplete)** folder.

Complete the program to:

- assign the string **"The book by Cami Stirrell is called 'The Hittomotapus'"** to variable **book**
- use the **index(<string>)** method to find the position in the string of the first single quote mark
- slice the string so that you can print the title of the book **'The Hittomotapus'**.

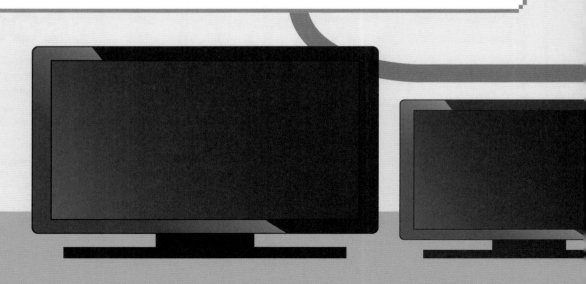

Validation routines

Validation of user input is often necessary to ensure that it is reasonable, or obeys certain rules.

Example 3

A user is asked to set a new password for an online application. The password must be at least 10 characters and must contain at least one uppercase letter and one lowercase letter.

```python
#Program name: Level 6 Example 3 Validate new password

print("Your password must be at least 10 characters long")
print("It must contain at least one uppercase and one lowercase letter")

validPassword = False

while not validPassword:
    validPassword = True
    password = input("Please enter password: ")
    if len(password) < 10:
        validPassword = False
        print("Must be at least 10 characters")
    if password.isupper():
        validPassword = False
        print("Must contain at least one lowercase letter")
    if password.islower():
        validPassword = False
        print("Must contain at least one uppercase letter")
    if not validPassword:
        print("Invalid password")
print("Valid password entered")
```

Challenge 95

Write a program which asks a user to enter a new password. The password must be at least 10 characters long and the user is repeatedly asked to re-enter a password if it is less than 10 characters.

Once the user has entered a valid password, the user is asked to verify it by entering it a second time. If it matches, the message "Password accepted" is printed. Otherwise an error message is printed and the program terminates.

Challenge 96

A car rental firm asks a customer to answer "Y" or "N" to the question "Are you aged 25 or over?". Write a Boolean expression using the string method **upper()** to check if the user response assigned to variable **response** is either "Y" or "y".

Using the string method isnumeric()

If a user is asked to enter an integer value and they enter a non-numeric character, the program will crash when it attempts to convert the input using `int()`. You can ensure that the value they enter is an integer using the Python built-in string method `isnumeric(<string>)`.

Example 4

The following statements ask a user to enter the number of guests invited to an event. If they do not enter a numeric value, the entry is rejected.

```
guests = input("Enter number of guests invited: ")
if guests.isnumeric():
    guests = int(guests)
else:
    print("You must enter a numeric value")
```

Challenge 97 ★ 📁

Flight numbers are assigned to all journeys by air.

In an airport terminal, the user is prompted to enter a flight code made up of a 2-letter airline code (uppercase) followed by 4 digits.

The program checks that the airline code is either "AA" or "BA". It then checks the last 4 digits to ensure they are numeric. Lowercase letters are accepted.

If the number is not valid, a message "Invalid flight number, please re-enter" is printed.

This is repeated until a valid flight number is entered. A message "Flight number accepted" is then printed.

The partially completed program is named **Challenge 97 Flight number incomplete**, saved in the **Starred challenges (incomplete)** folder.

Challenge 99 ★ 📁

Complete the program **Challenge 99 Event catering incomplete**, which calculates the catering requirements for an event. Ask the user to enter the number of number of guests invited. Validate the entry to ensure the number is numeric and in the range 1–75. If it is not, keep asking the user to re-enter until they enter a valid number. Then calculate and print the total requirements based on 8 party snacks per head.

Challenge 98 📖

The program code for **Challenge 98 Flight number incomplete** contains the condition

```
if not(flightNumber[0:2].upper() == "AA"
    or flightNumber[0:2].upper() == "BA"):
```

Explain the reason for using the method `upper()` in this statement.

Runtime errors

Example 5

The short program below is free of syntax and logic errors, but when it is executed, a **runtime error** occurs.

```
1  #Program name: Level 6 Example 5 Runtime error
2  #Example of a runtime error
3  myString = input("Please enter your surname: ")
4  #convert name to uppercase
5  myStringUppercase = mystring.upper()
6  print(myStringUppercase)
```

When the program is run, the following error message appears:

```
Please enter your surname: Smith
Traceback (most recent call last):
  File "C:/Level Example 5 a runtime error.py", line 5, in <module>
    myStringUppercase = mystring.upper()
NameError: name 'mystring' is not defined
```

Challenge 100

Python displays the line that had the error. Explain what the error is, and how to correct it.

Challenge 101

The following program runs correctly most of the time, but gives a runtime error when certain test data is used.

```
#Program name: Challenge 101 Example of a runtime error
powerGenerated = float(input("Total wind power generated Week 1 in kWh: "))
daysLowWind = int(input("Number of days with wind below 20mph: "))
daysWithWind = 7 - daysLowWind
averagePower = powerGenerated/daysWithWind
print("Average power generated on windy days:", averagePower))
```

Enter and run the program with test data. Identify two sets of test data that give different types of runtime error when the program is executed.

Formatting output

Printed output can be customised using the **format()** method. This is useful if, for example, you want output to appear in neat columns.

The **format()** method formats the specified values and inserts them into the placeholders, which are defined using curly brackets.

This allows you to specify the width of each field, and whether the data in the field should be left aligned, centred or right aligned.

Example 6

```
#Program name: Level 6 Example 6 Formatting output
#prints radioactive elements and their half lives in neatly lined up columns

element1 = "Einsteinium, Es"
atomicNumber1 = 99
halfLife1 = 471.65

element2 = "Mendelevium, Md"
atomicNumber2 = 101
halfLife2 = 51.5

#print heading
print("{:<20}{:>18}{:>25}".format("Element","Atomic Number","Half Life (Days)"))
#print data
print("{:<20}{:>12d}{:>25.2f}".format(element1,atomicNumber1,halfLife1))
print("{:<20}{:>12d}{:>25.2f}".format(element2,atomicNumber2,halfLife2))
```

Output:

```
Element                   Atomic Number             Half Life (Days)
Einsteinium, Es                      99                       471.65
Mendelevium, Md                     101                        51.50
```

:< left aligns the data within the amount of character space specified

:> right aligns the data within the amount of character space specified

:^ centres the data within the amount of character space specified

d   indicates a decimal integer

f   indicates a fixed point number

Example 7

The program below generates 20 random floating point numbers between 0 and 1. Using these numbers, random numbers between 0 and 200, and between 50 and 250 are generated. The three sets of numbers are printed in neat columns.

```
#Program name: Level 6 Example 7 Formatting printed columns
import random

for index in range (20):
    num1 = random.random()      #returns a random number between 0 and 1
    num2 = num1 * 200           #returns a random number between 0 and 200
    num3 = num1 * 200 + 50      #returns a random number between 50 and 250

    #print num1 to 4 decimal places,
    #num2 to 2 decimal places, num3 to 1 decimal place

    #each number occupies 20 spaces and is right aligned
    print("{:>20.4f}{:>20.2f}{:>20.1f}".format(num1,num2,num3))
```

Challenge 102

Write a program that allows a user to enter two numbers **area1** and **area2**, e.g. 2.347 and 1, representing average daily rainfall in two different areas. Print a heading, and print the numbers with two decimal places on one line, each in a 10-character space.

```
Enter average daily rainfall for area 1: 2.347
Enter average daily rainfall for area 2: 1
     Area1      Area2
      2.35       1.00
```

Challenge 103 ★

Load the program **Challenge 103 Strawberries incomplete** from the **Starred challenges (incomplete)** folder. Save it in your own folder, and complete the missing lines.

LEVEL 7
SUBROUTINES

Procedures and functions

Many programming languages have two types of subroutine, called functions and procedures, which are called in a slightly different way.

- A **procedure** may or may not take **parameters**. It carries out instructions but does not return a value. A parameter is a value that you input into, or pass to, a procedure or function.
- A **function** may or may not take parameters, but it always returns a value.

Built-in functions

Python has many built-in procedures and functions which you have already used. For example,

```
print("My name is ", myName)
```

calls a built-in **procedure** named **print()** which takes any number of parameters separated by commas. The parameters in this example are the string **"My name is "** and the variable **myName**.

```
myName = input("Please enter your name: ")
```

calls a built-in **function** named **input()** which displays an optional parameter (the prompt) and returns a value in **myName**.

> **! Tip**
>
> The range(start, stop, step) function is used to generate a list of numbers using step, beginning with the first and up to, but not including the last.
>
> float(), int(), str(), and len() are all examples of built-in functions which you have used.
>
> round(x,n) rounds x to the number of digits after the decimal, using the 0.5 rule.
>
> chr(*integer*) returns the string which matches the Unicode value of *integer*
>
> ord(*char*) returns the integer equivalent to the Unicode value of a single character.

Challenge 104

Write a statement which calls the built-in function **round()** to round **price1**, a floating point variable containing 5.327, to two decimal places and assign the result to **price2**. What is the value of **price2** after the statement has been executed?

Challenge 105

Write a statement using the **ord()** function to convert the ASCII / Unicode character "A" to its equivalent integer 65 and print it.

Write a statement using **chr()** to convert the integer 68 to its equivalent ASCII character and print it. What is printed?

Importing library modules

In addition to its built-in functions, Python has a library of files called **modules**, each containing a set of functions which you can import into your own program.

To use any Python module, you first have to import it into your program using the statement:

```
import modulename
```

Math module

To import the math module, write the following statement at the beginning of your program:

```
import math
```

Here are four functions included in the **math** module:

Function	Description	Example
math.pi	the constant pi	area = 10 * math.pi ** 2 returns 98.69604401089359 in area
math.sqrt(x)	returns the square root of x	a = sqrt(81) returns 9.0 in a
math.ceil(r)	returns r rounded up to the nearest integer	b = math.ceil(3.6) returns 4 in b
math.floor(r)	returns r rounded down to the nearest integer	c = math.floor(5.1) returns 5 in c

Challenge 106

Write statements using a `for..next` loop to print every third number between 0 and 99 inclusive.

Challenge 107

Write statements using the `math.pi` constant to calculate and print, correct to two decimal places, the circumference of a circle with radius 5.8. (Use the formula circumference = $2\pi r$)

Tip: Include the function `round(x, numplaces)`

Challenge 108

The depth of the water at various points in a harbour is measured by a device, accurate to two decimal places. A mapmaker wants to print each recorded depth rounded down to the nearest integer. For example, a recorded depth of 40.63 m will be printed as 40 m.

Write statements to calculate and print depths recorded by the device as 38.0 m and 53.9 m, to the nearest integers below the recorded values.

Write a program to ask the user to enter the area of ocean (in square nautical miles) scheduled for cleanup each day to clear it of plastic pollution. One vessel can cover 12 square nautical miles per day. Calculate the smallest whole number of vessels required to operate the cleanup.

Time module

`time.sleep(sec)` Suspends the current process for the given number of seconds, then resumes at the next line of the program.

Example 1

The program below simulates a pedestrian crossing countdown display, which displays 10 secs, 9 secs,.. down to 0 secs after the button is pressed.

The first statement, `import time`, is needed to import the `time` module from the Python library.

```
#Program name: Level 7 Example 1 Pedestrian crossing
#Program counts down seconds until light turns green

import time
print("Wait")
for seconds in range(10,0,-1):
    print(seconds, "seconds")
    time.sleep(1)
print("Walk")
```

Challenge 110

Copy the program shown in Example 1 above, save and run it. Improve it so that the last display before "Walk" says "1 second" not "1 seconds".

Challenge 111 ★

Complete the program **Challenge 111 Timer incomplete** in the **Starred challenges (incomplete)** folder.

Writing your own procedures and functions

As your programs get longer, it is useful to divide them up into a series of well-defined subroutines, each performing a specific task. These subroutines are then called from the main program as required.

The example below is a simple example of this. The main program asks the user to enter a number representing either the radius of a circle or the side of a square. The appropriate subroutine (function) is called to calculate and return the area of the specified shape.

A function must be placed above the call statement in a Python program so that the interpreter can read the function before it is called.

Example 2

```python
#Program name: Level 7 Example 2 area of a square or circle
#Calls functions to calculate area of a square or circle
import math

def square(side):
    area = side * side
    return area

def circle(radius):
    area = math.pi * radius ** 2
    return area

#main program
print("This program calculates the area of either a square or a circle\n")
myShape = input ("Enter a shape, S for square or C for circle: ")
shape = myShape.upper()
while shape != "S" and shape != "C":
    myShape = input("Please enter S or C: ")
    shape = myShape.upper()

#enter side or radius
if shape == "S":
    sideLength = float(input("Enter length of side: "))
    area = square(sideLength)         #this is a call statement
else:
    circleRadius = float(input("Enter radius: "))
    area = circle(circleRadius)       #this is another call statement

print("Area =",area)
```

A variation of the program in Example 2, named **Challenge 112 area of square, circle or triangle incomplete** is saved in the **Starred challenges (incomplete)** folder. Load it and add another option to calculate the area of a triangle. The user must enter the lengths of the base and the height. The formula for the area of a triangle is **½ base × height**. Amend each subroutine so that it returns the area rounded to two decimal places.

Example 3

Part of an incomplete program is shown below. A function named **menu** displays four choices and asks the user to select an option between 1 and 3. This is returned to the main program.

```
#Program name: Level 7 Example 3 Call menu subroutine

def menu():
    print("Menu options")
    print("1. Display rules")
    print("2. Start a new game")
    print("3. Quit")
    choice = input("Enter choice: ")
    return choice

#main program
option = menu()
#Program continues here…
#Try Challenge 113 to complete the rest of the program.
```

Execution starts at the first statement in the main program. This statement, `option = menu()`, calls a function named `menu()`, which displays a menu of options and returns the choice made by the user. Execution then continues at the next statement after the function call in the main program.

Note how the function is called. The variable `choice` from the subroutine is referred to as `option` in the main program. In this example, no parameters are passed to the function.

Challenge 113

Load the program **Level 7 Challenge 113 Call menu subroutine incomplete** from the **Starred challenges (incomplete)** folder. Add code to validate the choice within the function `menu()`. Complete the rest of the main program code, which calls functions for the different options chosen by the user. These functions are "stubs" which have not been written, but are there to test out the main program and its calls to the functions.

! Tip

This program illustrates the "top-down" approach to developing a program. The main program is written and tested first, calling function "stubs" which can each be developed and tested independently.

Challenge 114

Write a program which asks the user to input their first name and then calls a procedure which prints "Hello Jane" or whatever name is entered.

Challenge 115

Write a program which:

- asks a user to enter their firstname, surname, and date of birth in the format ddmmyy
- calls a subroutine which creates a username consisting of the first two letters of surname followed by first two letters of firstname (both in uppercase) and date of birth. For example, Thomas Vincent born 18/01/2005 will be given username VITH180105
  Tip: Use string slicing, concatenation and the method `string.upper()`. See Page 44.
- returns the username to the main program and prints it.

Challenge 116

Write a program which asks the user to enter in the format hhmmss the number of hours, minutes and seconds taken by a runner to complete a marathon. Call a subroutine to convert this time to a number of seconds. In the main program, print the number of seconds taken. (**Tip:** use string slicing.)

Test your program by entering a time of 2 hours, 1 minute and 1 second in the format 020101. The expected result is 7261 seconds.

What happens if you enter 211 instead of 020101?

! Tip

Download **syntaxsummary.py** from the Python programs folder ClearRevise.com for a Python version of the quick reference guide at the back of this book. It provides a useful example of a menu.

Local and global variables

Variables created outside a subroutine (procedure or function) are called **global variables**. They can be used in the main program and in any subroutines.

Example 4

```
#Program name: Level 7 Example 4 Global variables

def printGlobalName():
  print("Musketeer: " + musketeerName)
#end function

musketeerName = "Athos"
printGlobalName()
```

This will print **Musketeer: Athos**.

A **local variable** may be defined within a subroutine. It will take precedence over any variable of the same name used outside that subroutine.

Example 5

```
#Program name: Level 7 Example 5 Local variables

def printLocalName():
#A local variable defined within the function takes precedence
  musketeerName = "Porthos"
  print("Musketeer: " + musketeerName)

musketeerName = "Athos"
printLocalName()
```

This will print **Musketeer: Porthos**.

Example 6

You can declare a global variable inside a subroutine using the **global** keyword.

```
#Program name: Level 7 Example 6 Using global keyword

def defineGlobalName():
    global musketeerName
    musketeerName = "Aramis"

defineGlobalName()
print("Musketeer: " + musketeerName)
```

This will print **Musketeer: Aramis**.

Random module (import random)

`random.randint(a,b)` — returns a random integer X so that a <= X <= b

`random.random()` — returns a floating point number in the range 0.0 to 1.0

Challenge 117

Load the program **Challenge 117 Local and global variables** from the **Challenge Solutions\Level 7 Challenges** folder. Examine the code and run the program.

(a) Name **two** global variables used in the program.

(b) Name **four** local variables used in the function `simulation()`

(c) Explain the effect on execution of the program of uncommenting the statement `print(face)` in the main program.

Challenge 118

Write a statement to assign a random floating point number between 0 and 20 to the variable **seconds**.

Challenge 119

Write a program to generate and print 20 numbers between 30 and 100, rounded to 2 decimal places.
Print the average of all the numbers, rounded to two decimal places.

Challenge 120

Complete the program **Challenge 120 Random number test incomplete**. The program simulates throwing a 6-sided dice a number of times and prints how many times each face appears.

TURTLE GRAPHICS

The turtle module

The turtle module provides a simple graphics programming tool called the **turtle**.
The statement `import turtle` at the beginning of a program loads the module which provides all the turtle functionality.

A turtle is an object that the user can control. It can move forward or backward and turn in any direction. If its tail (the pen) is down, it draws a line of a specified colour and thickness.

Turtle functions

Some basic turtle functions you should be familiar with are given in the table below.

Function	Description
`turtle.forward(steps)`	Moves forward (facing direction) for the given number of steps
`turtle.back(steps)`	Moves backward (opposite-facing direction) for the number of steps
`turtle.left(degrees)`	Turns anticlockwise the number of degrees
`turtle.right(degrees)`	Turns clockwise the number of degrees
`turtle.home()`	Moves to canvas origin (0, 0)
`turtle.setpos(x, y)`	Positions the turtle at coordinates (x, y)
`turtle.reset()`	Clears the drawing canvas, sends the turtle home and resets variables to default values
`turtle.hideturtle()`	Makes the turtle invisible
`turtle.showturtle()`	Makes the turtle visible
`turtle.penup()`	Lifts the pen up
`turtle.pendown()`	Puts the pen down
`turtle.pensize(width)`	Makes the pen the size of **width** (positive number) e.g. 5
`turtle.pencolor(color)`	Sets the pen colour. The input argument can be a string or an RGB value. For example: "red", "#551A8B" or "(0,35,102)"
`turtle.setup(x, y)`	Specifies the size of the window where x = width in pixels, y = height in pixels. (Default is screen size.)
`turtle.circle(r)`	Draws a circle of radius r
`turtle.shape()`	Sets the turtle shape to the shape with a given name, e.g. `turtle.shape("turtle")`. The default shape `"classic"` is an arrowhead.

Example 1

Write a program to draw a small blue square on the screen.

```
#Program name: Level 8 Example 1 Introducing the turtle
import turtle

turtle.pensize(5)
turtle.pencolor("blue")

for n in range (4):
    turtle.forward(100)
    turtle.right(90)
```

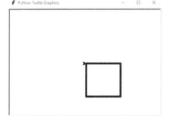

You can move the turtle to another position in the window with the statement:

```
turtle.setpos(x,y)
```

This moves the turtle to a position with coordinates `(x,y)`.

Python automatically adjusts the size of the window to fit your screen, but you can specify it yourself with the `setup()` function:

```
turtle.setup(800,600)
```

By default, the turtle is in the shape of an arrow, and starts off in the middle of the window, facing right. This is the position with coordinates `(0,0)`.

> **Tip**
>
> Before moving the turtle to a starting position, lift the pen with the statement
> ```
> turtle.penup()
> ```
> Before starting to draw:
> ```
> turtle.pendown()
> ```

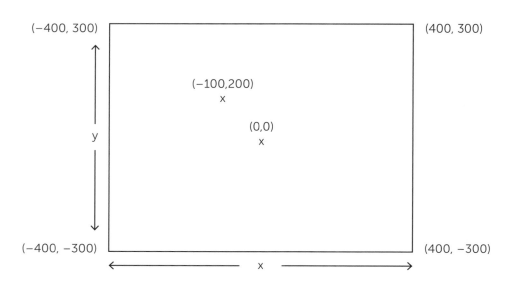

Copy the program given in Example 1. Then change the pen colour to green, pen width to 10 and move to a new start point with coordinates (–100, 200). Draw a hexagon with sides of length 75.

Write a program which sets the pen width to 3 and pen colour to red. Hide the turtle and draw a pentagon with sides of length 100 pixels, starting in the middle of the screen.

Complete the program **Challenge 123 Draw red shape incomplete** which sets the pen colour to red, the width to 10, the turtle to a turtle shape and the drawing speed to "slow". Draw the following shape on the screen, starting at coordinates (0,0) in the middle of the screen.

(Each square in the grid is 100 × 100 pixels).

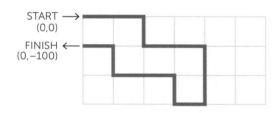

Write a program which sets the pen colour to blue, the width to 5. Draw the following shape on the screen, starting at coordinates (–100, –100). (Each square in the drawing is 100 × 100 pixels).

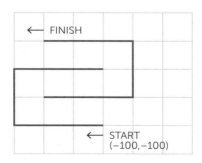

Challenge 125

Write a program to hide the turtle and position it at coordinates (–200, 100). Then use a **for** loop to draw five squares, each having sides 75 pixels, spaced 20 pixels apart in a horizontal line.

Challenge 126

A list of pen colours may be saved in a list with a statement such as

```
colour = ["red", "orange", "yellow", "green", "blue", "purple"]
```

Import the **random** module and use the **random.randint()** function to generate a random number between 0 and 5 to store in a variable named **index**. Draw a square with sides of length 100 pixels where each side is a random colour from the list.

Challenge 127

Write a program to draw 20 squares with each side in a random colour placed at randomly generated coordinates (x,y) where x and y are each between –200 and +200.

Challenge 128

The statement **turtle.circle(50)** draws a circle of radius 50. Write a program to hide the turtle and draw five overlapping red circles of radius 50:

Interacting with the user

The program may allow the user to select line colour and width, shape etc. All user interaction takes place in the Python Shell (interactive) window, as with other programs. The Shell window or the graphics window may be hidden, so just move it aside if necessary.

Example 2

A regular polygon is a flat shape whose sides are all equal and whose angles are all equal. The interior angle of a regular polygon with n sides is given by the formula **(n – 2) * 180 / n**

The procedure **drawPolygon(sideLength, numsides)** draws a regular polygon with **n** sides each of length **sideLength**.

```python
#Procedure to draw a regular polygon
def drawPolygon(sideLength, numSides):
    interiorAngle = (numSides - 2) * 180 / numSides
    turnAngle = 180 - interiorAngle

    #clear the drawing canvas, send the turtle home
    #and reset variables to default values
    turtle.reset()
    for n in range(numSides):
        turtle.forward(sideLength)
        turtle.right(turnAngle)
```

Challenge 129

Write a statement which calls the function **drawPolygon()** to draw an equilateral triangle with sides of length 100.

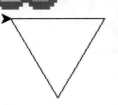

Challenge 130

Amend the function **drawPolygon()** so that it draws the polygon starting in a direction specified by the user. Name the amended function **drawPolygon2()** Call the function so that it draws a triangle with its flat base at the bottom.

(**Tip:** Start drawing at an angle of 60°)

Challenge 131 ★ 📁

Complete the program **Challenge 131 Select pen colour incomplete**. In the main program, the pensize is set to 10 and the starting position to (−100,200)

The program calls a function to allow the user to select a pen colour.

It then draws a pentagon with sides of length 100.

Challenge 132 ★ 📁

Complete the program **Challenge 132 Draw pattern of regular polygons incomplete**.

The program:

- allows the user to select the pen colour and pen width
- allows the user to specify the number of sides and length of each side
- calls a procedure `drawPolygon()` to draw the shape.

You are required to insert the three missing statements in the program.

Run the completed program several times with different polygons to create the interesting patterns that emerge.

LEVEL 9

SEARCHING AND SORTING

9

Searching and sorting are two very common applications in computing.

The bubble sort

The bubble sort is many times slower than other sorts for lists of more than a few items, but although it is not generally used in practice it is a good introduction to sorting.

It works by repeatedly going through the list to be sorted, swapping adjacent elements if they are in the wrong order.

Example 1

A list of 5 numbers 31, 14, 25, 49, 18 is to be sorted. Show the state of the list after each pass.

List	31	14	25	49	18	
Pass 1	14	31	25	49	18	
	14	25	31	49	18	
	14	25	31	49	18	
	14	25	31	18	49	Examine 5 items

> **! Tip**
>
> In some cases, the algorithm may sort the list before all the passes have been completed. The algorithm can check whether any swaps were made in the previous pass, and if not, the list is sorted and the algorithm can terminate.

After the first pass through the list, the largest number has 'bubbled' to the end of the list. In the second pass, we only need to compare the first four items.

Pass 2	14	25	31	18	49	
	14	25	31	18	49	
	14	25	18	31	49	Examine 4 items
Pass 3	14	25	18	31	49	
	14	18	25	31	49	Examine 3 items
Pass 4	14	18	25	31	49	Examine 2 items

The list is now sorted.

Example 2

```
#Program name: Level 9 Example 2 Bubble sort (fish)

fish = ["parrotfish", "grouper", "boxfish", "damselfish",\
        "snapper", "ray"]

#get number of items in the list
numItems = len(fish)
passNumber = numItems - 1
swapMade = True
while passNumber > 0 and swapMade:
    swapMade = False
    for j in range(passNumber):
        if fish[j] > fish[j + 1]:
            temp = fish[j]
            fish[j] = fish[j + 1]
            fish[j + 1] = temp
            swapMade = True
    passNumber = passNumber - 1
print("\nSorted list:\n",fish)
```

Challenge 133

How many passes will be required to sort the following list?

parrotfish, grouper, boxfish, damselfish, snapper, ray

Challenge 134

Load program **Challenge 134 Bubble sort incomplete** from the **Starred challenges (incomplete)** folder. Amend it so that it prints the state of the list and the value of the Boolean variable **swapMade** after each pass.

Explain why in this algorithm, the last pass does not always change the list.

Challenge 135

Make amendments to **Example 1 Bubble sort** so that it does not use the "flag", `swapsMade`, which indicates that the list is now sorted. How many passes are made through the list this time?

Challenge 136

Define a new list named `myList` of items in any sequence.

Write a statement to find the length of the list and assign it to `myListLength`.

Write a statement to assign the third item in the list to a variable named `temp`.

Challenge 137

Complete the program **Challenge 137 Sort earthquakes in descending order incomplete** that sorts a list of test data containing 10 randomly generated earthquake magnitudes between 0.0 and 10.0 on the Richter scale into descending numerical order.

Searching algorithms

The simplest kind of search is the **linear search**. Every item is examined from the beginning of a list of items until the one being searched for is found, or until every item in the list has been searched without finding it.

Example 3

```
#Program name: Level 9 Example 3 linear search
fish = ["parrotfish", "grouper", "boxfish", "damselfish",\
        "snapper", "ray"]
print("List of fish to be searched:", fish)
found = False
index = 0
searchItem = int(input("Enter a fish to look for: "))

while not found and index < len(fish):
    print(fish[index])
    if fish[index] == searchItem:
        found = True
    else:
        index = index + 1

if found:
    print(searchItem, "was found at position", index)
else:
    print("Item not found")
```

Challenge 138

The user searches for **"damselfish"** in the list in Example 3 above. Amend the **print** statement executed when the item is found, to print:

```
damselfish is item 4 in the list
```

Challenge 139

(a) In a list of 1000 items, how many items on average will need to be examined to find a particular item using a linear search?

(b) What is the maximum number of items that may need to be examined in a linear search, to find an item or report that it is not in the list?

Binary search

The linear search algorithm is useful for searching short lists. However, many lists in the real world contain thousands or even millions of items.

A binary search is a much more efficient search algorithm for searching a sorted list. It cannot be used on unsorted lists.

It works by repeatedly dividing in half the portion of the list that could contain the item. This continues until there is only one item left in the list.

Example 4

An ordered list of 12 numbers contains the following data items. To find whether the number 34 is in the list, start by examining the middle item in the list (this is the sixth item in this list of 12 numbers).

17	19	22	34	38	43	45	51	62	73	86	94

Stage 1: The search item 34 is less than 43. Discard all the items greater than or equal to 43.

19	19	22	34	38

Stage 2: The middle item is the third item, which is 22. 34 is greater than 22, so discard items less than or equal to 22.

34	38

Stage 3: The 'middle' item in a list of two numbers is the first one, 34. This is the number we are searching for, so the algorithm can report that the number has been found. If we had been searching for, say, 33, we would know at this stage that the number is not in the list.

34

Sometimes the search item is found before completing all the stages. If we had been searching for the number 43, we would have found it at Stage 1, its position in the list would be returned and the algorithm could then be made to terminate.

Challenge 140

Which items would be examined when looking for the name **Peter** in a binary search of the following list?

["Ava", "Fred", "George", "Jas", "Ken", "Lila", "Manesh", "Oliver", "Peter", "Tom"]

Example 5

The following program performs a binary search on a list of names to determine whether a particular name is in the list.

```python
#Program name: Level 9 Example 5 Binary search of names
#The list to be searched contains 10 names
aList = ["Ava", "Danesh", "Fred", "George", "Ishaan", "Jas", \
         "Ken", "Lila", "Manesh", "Oliver", "Peter", "Tabu"]
print("List of names to be searched:", aList)
found = False
first = 0
last = len(aList) - 1
searchItem = input("Enter number you are looking for: ")

while found == False and first <= last:
    midpoint = int((first + last) / 2)
    if aList[midpoint] == searchItem:
        found = True
        index = midpoint
    else:
        if aList[midpoint] < searchItem:
            first = midpoint + 1
        else:
            last = midpoint - 1
#endwhile
if found:
    print("Found at position", index,"in the list, starting at index 0")
else:
    print("Item is not in the list")
```

Challenge 141

What is the value of each of the following variables the first time the loop is executed?

(a) midpoint   (b) alist[midpoint]

Challenge 142 ★

Load the program **Challenge 142 Binary search** from the **Starred challenges (incomplete)** folder. Save it in your own folder, complete and execute it.

Insert a **print** statement which is printed each time the **while** loop is executed. How many times will the **print** statement within the loop be executed if the user searches for "Ben"? What will be the final line printed when the program is executed?

Challenge 143 ★ 📁

Complete the program **Challenge 143 Binary search of 1000 product numbers incomplete** which generates one thousand random integers for product numbers between 1 and 1000 and saves them in a list. The list is then sorted using Python's inbuilt `sort()` method.

Ask the user to enter a number to search for. Print all the numbers examined in a binary search of the numbers. Print a suitable message (e.g. "Found at position x" or "Item is not in the list" when the search ends.

Challenge 144 ★ 📁

Complete the program **Challenge 144 Computer guesses your number incomplete** which asks the user to think of a number between 1 and 1000 and write it down.

The program then guesses the number by asking questions such as:

"Is it less than, equal to or greater than 500?"

"Is it less than, equal to or greater than 250?"

Note that this version of the program contains no validation of the user's entry. In Challenge 147 you will test and check a similar program with an invalid user entry.

Types of error

You have come across several examples of three different types of error:

- Syntax errors
- Logic errors
- Runtime errors

Syntax errors are the easiest to find because Python highlights them when you try to run your program, and you can then correct them, save and try again.

Logic errors cause a program to operate incorrectly, but not necessarily to terminate abnormally. They may return a wrong answer or cause a program to loop endlessly. They can be very difficult to find.

Runtime errors occur when a program fails during execution and terminates abnormally with an error message. This is typically because a user has entered a value which the program does not cater for. A runtime error is caused by an illegal operation such as division by zero.

Detecting a logic error

A logic error is due to a fault in the algorithm and although the program may work correctly for some input, it may give wrong results for other possible input. Comprehensive testing is essential to ensure that the program works correctly for both valid and invalid data input.

Challenge 145

Load the program named **Challenge 145 Binary search with syntax errors**, from the **Starred challenges (incomplete)** folder. Locate and correct all the syntax errors.

Once all syntax errors have been removed, save and run the program, with a different name. Does it give correct results when you search for a bird name?

Some logic errors only come to light with comprehensive testing. For this reason, you should always test a program with data in the middle of the range, valid data just inside and just outside the boundaries of the expected range, invalid data and data of the wrong type, for example alphabetic characters instead of an integer.

Challenge 146 ★ 📖 📁

Here is the binary search program shown in Example 5 with just one logic error remaining.

```
#Program name: Challenge 146 Binary search with one logic error
#The list to be searched contains 12 names

aList = ["Ava", "Danesh", "Fred", "George", "Ishaan", "Jas", \
         "Ken", "Lila", "Manesh", "Oliver", "Peter", "Tabu"]

print("List of names to be searched:", aList)
found = False

#first is the index of the first name in the sublist to be searched
#last is the index of the last name in the sublist to be searched
first = 0
last = len(aList)

searchItem = input("Enter the name you are looking for: ")

#each time round the loop, either first or last is amended
#to specify a new sublist to be searched

while not found and first <= last:
    print("loop executed")
    midpoint = int((first + last) / 2)
    if aList[midpoint] == searchItem:
        found = True
        index = midpoint
    else:
        if aList[midpoint] < searchItem:
            first = midpoint + 1
        else:
            last = midpoint - 1

#endwhile
if found:
    print("Found at position " + str(index) + " in the list, starting at 0")
else:
    print("Item is not in the list")
```

Test the program (saved in the **Starred Challenges (incomplete)** folder) using the test plan in Table 1 on the next page. Fill in the column "Actual outcome" for each test.

Is it as expected in each case? If not, which test outcome is not as expected?

Test plan

Test purpose	Test data	Expected outcome	Actual outcome
Test mid-range data	Jas	List of names printed "Found at position 5 in the list, starting at 0"	As expected
Test lower boundary data	Ava	List of names printed "Found at position 0 in the list, starting at 0"	
Test upper boundary data	Tabu	List of names printed "Found at position 11 in the list, starting at 0"	
Test below boundary data	Anna	List of names printed "Item is not in the list"	
Test above boundary data	Vic	List of names printed "Item is not in the list"	

Table 1

Find and correct the error, then retest your program.

Challenge **147**

Load the program **Challenge 147 Test a program** from the **Challenge solutions** folder.

Complete the test plan for this program. Test the program with each input, and fill in the actual outcome of each test. Add two more tests of your own.

Is the actual outcome the same as the expected outcome in each case? It should not crash, whatever the user enters, and it should always give the correct result.

Test purpose	Test data	Expected outcome	Actual outcome
Test invalid number below lower boundary	0		As expected
Test upper boundary data	100		
Test middle of range data	50		

Table 2

READING AND WRITING TEXT FILES

The programs that you have written so far sometimes use data entered by the user. When the program ends, the data is lost.

Data often needs to be stored on a permanent storage device such as hard disk or SSD, so that it can be read and processed as often as required.

Most real-life applications will store data in a database, from which information can be easily retrieved using queries written in a language called SQL (Structured Query Language).

In this level you will practise reading from and writing to **text files**. A text file can be created in Python (see Level 10 Example 1a in the Examples folder), or even in Notepad. Each line in the file is a separate **record**, usually consisting of several **fields** of different data types. There are several different ways, in Python, to read records sequentially from a text file.

Reading a text file using `for <line> in <fileid>`

Example 1

A text file has been created to hold the names, genders and ages of seven students going on a outdoor survival weekend.

The program below opens the text file, reads all the records, prints them and closes the file.

```
#Program name: Level 10 Example 1 print text file
#reads records from a file named students1.txt and prints each record
studentFile = open("students1.txt","r")
for studentRec in studentFile:
    print(studentRec)
studentFile.close()
```

When this program is executed, the output is double-spaced:

```
Diaz,Rosa,F,15

Hamilton,Jerome,M,16

Head,Jennifer,F,16

(etc.)
```

📄 students1.txt - Notepad

File   Edit   Format   View   Help

```
Diaz,Rosa,F,15
Hamilton,Jerome,M,16
Head,Jennifer,F,16
Robinson,Keith,M,15
Zelter,Cordelia,F,16
Kelly,Jason,M,16
Browne,Gary,M,15
```

Opening, reading and closing a text file

In Example 1, the **open** statement assigns the file pathname **student1.txt** to the variable **studentfile**. This file is saved in the same folder as the program and is referred to by this name in the program.

In the **open** statement, the parameter **"r"** indicates that the file is to be opened in **read** mode. In this mode, it is not possible to write or change a record.

The file is closed with the statement **studentFile.close()**. You should always include this statement. It ensures that the file is ready to be reopened, if necessary, in a different mode. If the file is opened in **write** mode, it ensures that all data written to the file is saved.

The invisible newline character

When a file is created in Notebook, every time you press the **Enter** key, an invisible newline character **\n** is added to the end of the line.

The output in Example 1 is double-spaced because each time a **print** statement is executed, the output is automatically followed by a line break. The invisible newline character at the end of each record causes an additional line break.

Challenge 148

Copy the program **Level 10 Example 1 print text file**, save it and run it. Use **students1.txt** stored in the **Examples** folder. Check that the output is as shown on the previous page.

Now try amending the **print** statement to **print(studentRec, end = "")**

The **end = ""** parameter prevents the automatic line break after a **print** statement is executed.

Tip

The **read()** method is another way of reading a whole file:

```
studentFile = open("students1.txt","r")
print(studentFile.read())
studentFile.close()
```

Challenge 149

Create and save a new file in Notepad named **country.txt** with three records each holding a country name. Press **Enter** after the last record. Include a blank line at the end of the file. (This ensures that there is a newline character **\n** at the end of the last record.)

Save the file in your program folder. Write a program to open the file, read each record in the file and print it on a separate line, single spaced, and close the file.

Accessing individual fields (using `split(<char>)`)

In the text file **student1.txt**, individual fields in each record are separated by commas. In Example 2 these fields will be named **surname, firstname, gender, age**. To access these individual fields, the **split(<char>)** method is used, specifying a comma as the field separator.

Tip

The `split(<char>)` method returns a list of all substrings in the original text, using `<char>` as the separator

The `strip(<char>)` method returns the original string with all occurrences of char removed from the front and back. It is used here to remove the invisible newline character \n from the last field in each line.

Example 2

```
#Program name: Level 10 Example 2 split and strip methods
#reads every line from a file named students1.txt

studentFile = open("students1.txt","r")

for studentRec in studentFile:
#split the record into individual fields
#comma is the field separator
    field = studentRec.split(",")
    surname = field[0]
    firstname = field[1]
    gender = field[2]
    age = field[3]
#strip newline character from last field
    age = age.strip("\n")
    print(firstname, surname, "is", age, "years old")

studentFile.close()
```

This produces the following output:

```
Rosa Diaz is 15 years old
Jerome Hamilton is 16 years old
Jennifer Head is 16 years old
Keith Robinson is 15 years old
Cordelia Zelter is 16 years old
Jason Kelly is 16 years old
Gary Browne is 15 years old
```

Using `readline()` to read a file

Instead of using a **for** loop to process a file, you can read each line individually using the syntax:

```
<aline> = <fileid>.readline()
```

This returns a line from the file. On reaching the end of file it returns an empty string.

Example 3

```python
#Program name: Level 10 Example 3 Use readline() to read male students

#read records from a file named students1.txt
studentFile = open("students1.txt","r")

#Print all male student records
endOfFile = False
while not endOfFile:
    studentRec = studentFile.readline()
    #returns an empty string on the end of file
    if studentRec == "":
        endOfFile = True
    else:
    #split the record into individual fields
    #comma is the field separator
    fieldList = studentRec.split(",")
    surname = fieldList[0]
    firstname = fieldList[1]
    gender = fieldList[2]
    age = fieldList[3]
    if gender == "M":
        print(surname, firstname, gender, age, end = "")

studentFile.close()
```

This produces the following output:

```
Hamilton Jerome M 16
Robinson Keith M 15
Kelly Jason M 16
Browne Gary M 15
```

Using `readlines()` to read a file

The **`readlines()`** method, unlike the **`readline()`** method, reads the entire file using a single statement. It returns a list in which each item is a line from the file.

Example 4

```
#Program name: Level 10 Example 4 Use readlines() to print student list
#<alist> = <fileid>.readlines() returns a list
#where each item is a line from the file

studentFile = open("students1.txt","r")

studentList = studentFile.readlines()

print("Print studentList")
print(studentList)
print("\n\nPrint each element of the list\n")

for nameString in studentList:
   print(nameString, end = "")

studentFile.close()
```

This produces the following output:

```
Print studentList
['Diaz,Rosa,F,15\n', 'Hamilton,Jerome,M,16\n', 'Head,Jennifer,F,16\n',
 'Robinson,Keith,M,15\n', 'Zelter,Cordelia,F,16\n', 'Kelly,Jason,M,16\n',
 'Browne,Gary,M,15\n']

Print each element of the list

Diaz,Rosa,F,15
Hamilton,Jerome,M,16
Head,Jennifer,F,16
Robinson,Keith,M,15
Zelter,Cordelia,F,16
Kelly,Jason,M,16
Browne,Gary,M,15
```

Challenge 150

Load the program **Challenge 150 split and strip methods** from the folder **Python programs\ Challenge solutions\Level 10 Challenges**. Run the program.

Comment out the line

```
age = age.strip("\n")
```

Save and run the program. What is the output?

Challenge 151

Copy the incomplete program **Challenge 151 print male students aged 15 incomplete** and the text file **student1.txt** from the **Starred challenges (incomplete)** folder.

Complete the program, save in your own folder and test it.

Challenge 152

Mrs Lopez is selling items that have been stored in her garage.

Copy the incomplete program **Challenge 152 Use readline()** and the text file **Items for sale.txt** into your folder.

The program should:

- open the text file **Items for sale.txt** in **read** mode
- read the text file
- split the record into individual fields
- find the total sale price of all items
- print the items and the total sale price

Challenge 153

A student has created a text file in Notepad to record all the birds observed on a trip.

The file is named **myBirds.txt** and is stored in the **Starred challenges (incomplete)** folder.

Copy the incomplete program **Challenge 153 Read myBirds.txt file and sort names incomplete** and the text file **myBirds.txt** into your own folder.

Complete the program. Save it and run it.

Modes in the open statement

It is not possible to delete or amend records in a text file directly from within a program. Records can be written to a new file or appended to the end of an existing file.

The mode specified in the **open** statement opens the file for **reading** an existing file, **writing** to a new file (or overwriting an existing one), or **appending** records to an existing file.

Operation	Mode
Read records from an existing file	"r"
Create a new file and write records to the file	"w"
Append new records to the end of an existing file	"a"

Appending data to an existing file

To add more data to the end of an existing file, open the file in **append** mode.

```
studentFile = open("students group1.txt","a")
```

This will append data to the end of an existing file, or create a new file if the named file does not exist or cannot be found.

You can create a new file, or overwrite all the data in an existing file, by opening it in **write mode**.

 **Example 5**

The program below appends new records for Marshall,Diana,F,15, and Davis,Clive,M,14 to a copy of the file **students1.txt**. The copy is named **students2.txt**.

```
#Program name: Level 10 Example 5 append records
#appends records to students2.txt
#This is a copy of the original students1.txt

studentFile = open("students2.txt","a")

#Accept data from user
moreStudents = True
while moreStudents:
    surname = input("Enter surname, xxx to end: ")
    if surname == "xxx":
        moreStudents = False
    else:
        firstname = input("Enter firstname: ")
        gender = input("Enter 'M' or 'F': ")
        age = input("Enter age: ")
        studentFile.write(surname + "," + firstname + "," \
                          + gender + "," + age + "\n")

studentFile.close()
```

The table below shows some of the countries which generate a significant amount of renewable electricity.

Renewable energy statistics December 2020

Country	Wind (GW)	Solar (GW)	Hydro (GW)	% Renewable energy
Brazil	14.5	3.87	350	75
Germany	59.3	49.8	11.3	46
Spain	23.5	8.7	17	45
China	221	130	360	40
UK	20.7	13.4	11.2	47
France	15.3	9.43	25.5	33
USA	96.4	71.3	273.7	24
India	35	28.18	45.7	38

The data is stored in a text file named **renewables2020.txt** in the folder **Challenge solutions\Level 10 challenges**. There are eight records, each consisting of five fields. The fields are separated by commas, and each record starts on a new line.

Write a program to read the text file and print all the records.

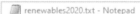

```
renewables2020.txt - Notepad
File  Edit  Format  View  Help
Brazil,14.5,3.87,350,75
Germany,59.3,49.8,11.3,46
Spain,23.5,8.7,17,45
China,221,130,360,40
UK,20.7,13.4,11.2,47
France,15.3,9.43,25.5,33
USA,96.4,71.3,273.7,24
India,35,28.18,45.7,38
```

Using the format() method

In Level 6, page 51, the formatting of output was covered. The following program reads and prints each record in the **renewables2020.txt** file, formatting the output in neat columns.

Example 6

```
#Program name: Level 10 Example 6 Print renewables file formatted in columns

energyFile = open("renewables2020.txt","r")
endOfFile = False
#print headings
print("Country     Wind     Solar     Hydro     Percent renewables")
while not endOfFile:
    energyRec = energyFile.readline()
    if energyRec == "":
        endOfFile = True
    else:
        #split the record into individual fields
        #comma is the field separator
        fieldList = energyRec.split(",") #comma is the field separator
        country = fieldList[0]
        wind = float(fieldList[1])
        solar = float(fieldList[2])
        hydro = float(fieldList[3])
        percentRenewables = float(fieldList[4])

        #The format() method allows you to print in neat columns
        print("{:10}{:8.2f}{:8.2f}{:8.2f}{:8.1f}"\
            .format(country,wind,solar,hydro,percentRenewables))
```

Congratulations, you've finished!

```
Country      Wind    Solar   Hydro    % renewables
Brazil      14.50     3.87   350.00       75.0
Germany     59.30    49.80    11.30       46.0
Spain       23.50     8.70    17.00       45.0
China      221.00   130.00   360.00       38.3
UK          20.70    13.40    11.20       28.1
France      15.30     9.43    25.50       19.6
USA         96.40    71.30   273.70       11.0
India       35.00    28.18    45.70        9.0
```

Challenge 155

Write a program to read the text file **renewables2020.txt** and print the amount of wind power generated in each country. Format the output to one decimal place in two columns with decimal points aligned.

```
Wind power generated in each country
Brazil          14.5
Germany         59.3
Spain           23.5
China          221.0
UK              20.7
France          15.3
USA             96.4
India           35.0
```

ANSWERS

Note: All programmed solutions are in subfolders of the Python programs folder. Download free from clearrevise.com.

Challenge 1:   `print("Gorillas are the largest living primates.")`

Challenge 2:   `print('The scientific name for the Western Lowland \`
                 `gorilla is "Gorilla gorilla gorilla"')`

Challenge 3:   `print("Don't worry.\nBe happy")`

Challenge 5:   Missing quote at end of line. The 'EOL while scanning string literal message' means the debugger reached the End Of Line while scanning the text string and couldn't find an end quote.
                 firstName = input("What is your name?)

Challenge 7:   `animal1`, `animal2` or `animal3` (or alternative variable names that you used)

Challenge 9:   All valid except (c) 1stClass and (f) A–1

Challenge 10:   `10 5`

Challenge 11:   `Fred Tom Fred`

Challenge 13:   (a) Max lives could be a constant in a computer game. (b) Lives remaining will vary during a computer game. (c) Population can vary over time. (d) The unit of gravity on earth is a constant.

Challenge 14:   ```
>>> firstname = input("Enter firstname: ")
Enter firstname: Jo
>>> surname = input("Enter surname: ")
Enter surname: Brown
>>> print(surname,firstname)
Brown Jo
>>>
```

Challenge 16:    (a) Missing quote at the end of a string. (**EOL** stands for End Of Line.)
                 (b) Incorrectly spelt or undefined variable name.

Challenge 18:    `print("13685 divided by 27 =",13687//27, " remainder ",`
                 `13687%27)`
                 *Result: 13685 divided by 27 = 506 remainder 23*

Challenge 19:    ```
mondayMiles = 20.0
tuesdayMiles = 23.75

print("Total miles travelled on Monday and Tuesday =",\
mondayMiles + tuesdayMiles)
```

Challenge 20:   `print((7*3) + (16/5))`

Challenge 21:   `print("2 to the power 10 =",2**10)`

Challenge 24:   (a) integer   (b) string   (c) float

Challenge 27:   Fahrenheit and Celsius temperatures are the same at −40

Challenge 28:   ```
>>> num1 = 24
>>> num2 = 3
>>> print("The sum of " + str(num1) + " and " + str(num2) + " is " + str(num1 +
    num2))
The sum of 24 and 3 is 27
```
```

Challenge 30:
```
x = input("Enter value for x : ")
y = input("Enter value for y : ")
temp = x
x = y
y = temp
print("Swapped values: x =",x, "  y =", y)
```

Challenge 33: 20

Level 3

Challenge 34:
```
>>> 10 * 7 == 70
True
```

Challenge 35:
```
>>> "John" != "JOHN"
True
```

Challenge 36:
```
>>> (6 <= 2*4) and (28 <= 7*4)
True
```

Challenge 37:
```
>>> (x < 0) and (y < 0)
```

Challenge 38:
```
>>> (x == 0) or (b == 0)
```

Challenge 39:
```
>>> a = 24/8
>>> b = 24 + 8
>>> print(a==b)
False
```

Challenge 40:
```
>>> print(237//17 == 237/17)
False
```

Challenge 41:
```
>>> print(10 == 5*2 and 45 != 9*5)
False
```

Challenge 42:
```
>>> print(6*3 >= 9*2 or 30//7 == 2)
True
```

Challenge 51: For example, use test data such as:
A, x (Invalid data, expected result – runtime error)
B, 109 (Boundary data, expected result "Failed. Requires adjustment." message)
D, 120 (invalid model data, valid decibel data. Expected result error message "Model must be A, B or C. No result given.")

Level 4

Challenge 56: These are some sample tests that you could use:

Test	a	b	Expected result	Actual result
1	3	26	13, 26	
2	3	27	13, 26	
3	13	39	13, 39	
4	12	45	13, 39	
5	−30	0	−29, −13, 0	
6	−40	−13	−39, −26, −13	
7	27	13	nothing printed	

Challenge 64:
```
Enter -1 when no more data
Enter number of lengths on day 1: ( etc)
```

Answers

Challenge 71:   `print(planet)`

Challenge 76:   `totals = [0] * 100`

Challenge 82:   `booking[1][2] = 96`

Challenge 87:   **20**

Challenge 88:   **7**   The "escape sequence" `\n` is counted as one character..

Challenge 89:
```
name = input("Enter full name")
print(len(name))
print(name[0])
print(name[len(name) - 1])
```

Challenge 96:   `response.upper() == "Y"`

Challenge 98:   It converts the characters entered by the user to uppercase. This means that the user can enter "aa", "AA", "Aa", "ba", etc. for the flight number to be accepted.

Challenge 100: `myStringUppercase = mystring.upper()`   is incorrect. It should be:
`myStringUppercase = myString.upper()` (Note the 'S' in `myString`.)

Challenge 101: Test data1: powerGenerated = abc (non-numeric value)
Test data 2: powerGenerated = 75, daysLowWind = 7 (division by zero)

Challenge 104: `price2 = round(price1,2)` assigns 5.33 to `price2`

Challenge 105:
```
print(ord("A"))
print(chr(68)) prints D
```

Challenge 106:
```
for n in range(0,100,3):
    print(n)
```

Challenge 107:
```
import math
area = 2 * math.pi*5.8
print(round(area,2))
```
(prints 36.44)

Challenge 108:
```
import math
print(math.floor(38.0))
print(math.floor(53.9))
```

Challenge 116: Python will report a runtime error when it reaches the line
`secs = int(time[4:6])`

Challenge 117: (a) Global variables: `title` (defined as `global` in the function) `heading` (declared in the main program)
(b) Local variables `face`, `n`, `dieroll`, `dieface`
(c) A runtime error will occur as the local variable `face` is only recognised within the function.

Challenge 118: `seconds = random.random()* 20`

Challenge 129: `drawPolygon(100,3)`

Challenge 133: Two passes, and an extra pass to verify that no swaps were made in the previous pass

Challenge 134: The Boolean variable **swapMade** is set to False if no swaps are made during a pass. The **while** loop then terminates.

Challenge 135: 5 passes though the list of 6 items

Challenge 136:
```
myList = [3,7,1,9,4,6]
myListLength = len(myList)
temp = myList[2]
```

Challenge 138: `print(searchItem, "was item", index + 1, "in the list")`

Challenge 139: (a) 500   (b) 1000

Challenge 140: Ken Oliver Peter

Challenge 141: (a) `midpoint = 5`   (b) `alist[midpoint] = "Jas"`

Challenge 142: **print** statement executed four times within loop.
Final **print** statement:
`Item is not in the list`

Challenge 145: Challenge 145 binary search with errors (in Starred Challenges (incomplete) folder).

Syntax errors:
`print("loop executed)`   missing quote mark
`else`   missing colon

Logic errors:
`midpoint = (firstIndex + lastIndex) / 2` should be int((first + last) / 2)
`lastIndex = len(aList)`   should be last = len(aList − 1)

Runtime errors:
`print("List of names to be searched:",aList[12])`
list index out of range
`print("Found at position" + index + "in….`
should be str(index) or use comma instead of +

Challenge 146: The last test results in a runtime error
`if aList[midpoint] == searchItem:`
`IndexError: list index out of range`
This is because **lastindex** should be initialised as **last = len(aList) - 1**

Challenge 147: Actual outcome should be as expected for all tests.
You could add tests to test the lower boundary data (1), test outside the top boundary (101), and test an invalid input (not <, =, or >).

Challenge 150: `Output will be:`
`Rosa Diaz is 15`
` years old`
`Jerome Hamilton is 16`
` years old`
etc.

PYTHON SYNTAX GUIDE

 Help

Download **syntaxsummary.py** from the Python programs folder available from **www.ClearRevise.com** for a Python version of this quick reference guide.

Input statement

```python
name = input("Enter name: ")
visitors = int(input("How many visitors? "))
cost = float(input("Enter cost per person: "))
totalCost = visitors * cost
```

Output statement

```python
print("Total cost:",totalCost)
```

or use concatenation to join two strings:

```python
print("TotalCost " + str(totalCost))
```

"end" parameter prevents automatic newline

```python
print("Total cost ",end="")
print(totalCost)
```

newline character **"\n"** causes a skip to a new line

Arithmetic operators

			Result
addition	a = 15 + 2	a = 17
subtraction	b = 15 - 2	b = 13
multiplication	c = 15 * 2	c = 30
division	d = 15 / 2	d = 7.5
exponentiation	e = 5 ** 2	e = 25
integer division (div)	f = 15 // 2	f = 7
remainder (mod)	g = 15 % 2	g = 1

Logical and Boolean operators

		Examples (a = 3, b = 5)	
less than	<	a < b	True
greater than	>	a > b	False
less than or equal	<=	a <= b	True
greater than or equal	>=	a >= b	False
equal	==	a == b	False
not equal	!=	a != b	True
logical and	and	a == b and b == 5	False
logical or	or	a == b or b == 5	True
logical not	not	not(a == b)	True

Definite iteration

print numbers 0 to 5:
```python
for n in range(6):
    print(n)
```

print numbers 5 to 8:
```python
for n in range(5,9):
    print(n)
```

print every third number between 1 and 10:
```python
for n in range(1,11,3):
    print(n)
```

print every third number counting down from 99 to 90, counting down
```python
for n in range(99,89,-3):
    print(n)
```

Indefinite iteration

```python
daysRemaining = 6
while daysRemaining > 0:
    daysRemaining = daysRemaining - 1
    print("Days to Christmas",\
        daysRemaining)
print("Happy Christmas!")
```

Selection

if statement
```python
if (age < 18):
    print("Under age")
```

if...else statement
```python
if (score >= 50):
    print("Pass")
else:
    print("Fail")
```

if...elif...else statement
```python
if (score >= 80):
    print("Well done")
    print("Distinction")
elif (score >= 70):
    print("Merit")
elif (score >= 50):
    print("Pass")
else:
    print("Fail")
```